# UNDERSTNDING DIABETES

## A COMPREHENSIVE GUIDE FOR PATIENTS

DR SHIV KUMAR LATH | MBBS | MD | FEAC

In humble reverence to the divine inspiration bestowed by Almighty Shiv Baba, it is with profound gratitude and spiritual guidance that I dedicate this "Handbook of Diabetes for Patients." May the wisdom and strength derived from His divine presence infuse this work, offering solace, support, and empowerment to those navigating the complexities of diabetes. In dedicating this book to the spiritual source of inspiration, I hope to share the transformative journey towards holistic well-being with the blessings of Shiv Baba.

# Contents


*Preface*                                                          *vii*

*Acknowledgements*                                            *xi*

*About The Author*                                           *xiii*

1. DEFINITION OF DIABETES MELLITUS            1

2. CLASSIFICATION                                                  3

3. ETIOLOGY                                                             5

4. DIAGNOSIS                                                            8

5. SCREENING OF DIABETES                               12

6. MANAGEMENT                                                     14

7. CLINICAL AND LAB EVALUATION OF A         50
   DIABETES PATIENT

8. COMPLICATIONS OF DIABETES                       56

9. DIABETES IN PREGNANCY                               93

10. DISEASES ASSOCIATED WITH DIABETES      103

11. UNDERSTANDING DIABETES REVERSAL     111

CONCLUSION                                                          113

CONNECT THROUGH BELOW MENTIONED LINK  115
WITH US

# Preface

Welcome to the "Handbook of Diabetes," a guide crafted by Dr. S.K. Lath, a compassionate diabetologist dedicated to simplifying the complexities of diabetes for patients. This book is not just a medical manual; it's a conversation in simple language, aimed at empowering individuals to navigate their diabetes journey with confidence.

Let us understand why you should read this book

Despite the abundance of information online about diabetes, complications such as heart attacks and kidney failure are on the rise due to various factors, including:

1. Inability to differentiate between accurate and misleading online information.

2. Blindly following advice from other patients, relying on questionable sources, and making incorrect decisions in diabetes management.

3. Confusion stemming from the overwhelming amount of information, with opinions varying across different websites and videos.

4. Lack of clarity on the treatment goals for diabetes and ignorance about its various complications.

5. Ignorance regarding the irreversibility of complications associated with Diabetes mellitus.

6. Dependence solely on symptoms, neglecting crucial parameters like blood sugar levels and other vital body indicators.

7. Limited practical knowledge amidst the multitude of online diabetes-related forums and discussions.

8. Permanently stopping the medications based on others' advice.

9. Fear of diabetes medications and insulin, coupled with a lack of knowledge on their proper usage.

10. Insufficient information about lifestyle changes essential for diabetes management, accompanied by fear and phobia related to diabetes mellitus in pregnancy.

Beyond these challenges, this book aims to address and solve multiple problems faced by individuals with diabetes. It is designed to keep diabetic patients healthy and happy for an extended duration by providing proper and concise knowledge.

1. This book is not a textbook and is not intended for doctors or pharmacists; it is specifically for patients and their caregivers.

2. It will eliminate confusion between different types of diabetes mellitus and offer tips for differentiation.

3. The book presents an easy-to-understand method for diagnosing and treating diabetes mellitus.

4. It emphasises the importance of regular checkups for diabetes patients and guides them on self-monitoring.

5. It provides knowledge about the aetiology of diabetes mellitus and offers preventive measures.

6. The book assists patients in creating their own diet charts, guiding them on food choices to manage diabetes.

7. Readers can learn from mistakes made by others through the "Meets and Mistakes" section in each chapter, helping them control blood sugar levels.

8. Patients will gain insight into drugs and insulin in simple language, covering dosage, side effects, and administration methods.

9. A dedicated chapter addresses gestational diabetes mellitus, aiding pregnant individuals in controlling blood sugar levels and ensuring a positive pregnancy outcome.

10. Patients will acquire knowledge about different diseases associated with diabetes mellitus and their management.

At the conclusion of each chapter, I've shared my experiences in Boulder or Italics or coloured text. I strongly recommend patients to carefully go through these insights.

With this book, patients can rest assured that they are receiving accurate and relevant information, enabling them to manage their diabetes effectively and avoid any complications.

The book is written in simple English language and Hindi too, so that any patient can easily understand and take actions from the advice given in the book.

Please note that this book is not a substitute for a textbook and may not contain the most recent data or facts. It is intended to explain the subject matter to patients in a simple manner, without complicated medical terms or language.

I have also shared my personal experience and emphasised practical points and mistakes that a patient may make in diabetes management which are not found in any textbook or patient manual.

It is my hope that this book will help all diabetes patients to understand the disease and the practical problems they face in their day-to-day life.

We aspire for this book to become a valuable addition to the libraries of both diabetes patients and physicians. It is accessible in both Hindi and English, allowing patients to choose the version that aligns with their reading preferences and comfort.

# Acknowledgements

In the pages of this "Handbook of Diabetes for Patients," I am profoundly grateful for the invaluable support and inspiration from a multitude of sources. To my esteemed teachers, your guidance has been the cornerstone of my knowledge, shaping this comprehensive resource. To my patients, your resilience and trust have fueled my commitment to providing essential information.

My heartfelt appreciation goes to my parents, whose unwavering support has been my bedrock. To my cherished wife Dr Dolly Lath, your understanding and encouragement have made this journey possible. To my children Rajnandini,Mriganka and Hrishiraj, your presence is my daily motivation and joy.

A special acknowledgment to the dedicated clinic staff, whose tireless efforts contribute to the well-being of our patients. The collaborative spirit within the clinic is reflected in every page of this handbook.

To the vibrant YouTube community, your engagement and shared experiences have enriched the conversation around diabetes awareness. Thank you for being an integral part of this journey.

This handbook is a testament to the collective effort and support of these individuals and communities. Your influence is woven into every word, and I am profoundly grateful for the collaborative spirit that has made this resource possible.

# About The Author

Dr. S.K. Lath, MD, FEAC, stands as a distinguished diabetologist and physician hailing from Jharsuguda, India. With a wealth of expertise in the field, he has contributed significantly to the medical community. His commitment to patient education led him to pen a comprehensive "Handbook of Diabetes for Patients," providing invaluable insights into managing diabetes effectively.

Beyond the confines of his medical profession, Dr. Lath wears multiple hats driven by his passion for diverse interests. A dynamic individual, he is a recognized singer, avid biker, compelling public speaker, and a profound philosopher. His multifaceted approach extends beyond the conventional realms of medicine, reflecting a holistic view of life.

In the digital sphere, Dr. Lath has taken to YouTube, utilising the platform to spread awareness about various diseases. Through informative content, he reaches a broader audience, aiming to empower individuals with knowledge about their health.

Adding another feather to his cap, Dr. Lath authored a book titled "15 Secrets to Crack Any Exam," providing a glimpse into his life's journey. This biography serves not only as a personal narrative but also as a guide, elucidating key lessons drawn from the author's mistakes and learning. Dr. Lath's commitment to education, both in the medical and broader life context, exemplifies his dedication to fostering a healthier, more informed society.

YOU CAN BUY THE BOOK ONLINE FROM BELOW MENTIONED ADDRESS

**English Edition:**

Get your paperback copy in India: [15 Secrets to Crack Any Exam]

BY SEARCHING THE BOOK TITLE IN nOTION PRESS WEBSITE

For paperback overseas, visit: [Amazon - Paperback](https://www.amazon.com/SECRETS-CRACK-ANY-EXAM-AUTOBIOGRAPHY/dp/B0CN1XXBLM/ref=tmm_pap_swatch_0?_encoding=UTF8&qid=&sr=)

Explore the e-book version on Amazon: [E-Book](https://www.amazon.com/dp/B0CN3TB89G/ref=tmm_kin_swatch_0?_encoding=UTF8&qid=&sr=)

**Hindi Edition:**

Grab the paperback version: [15 Secrets to Crack Any Exam in Hindi BY SEARCHING THE BOOK TITLE IN nOTION PRESS WEBSITE

For the e-book in Hindi, check out: [Amazon - Hindi E-Book](https://www.amazon.com/dp/B0CN3SJPNY)

You can explore his clinic at following online address

Explore Dr. Lath Polyclinic on Google by visiting: https://g.page/r/CfF9aWzdVvOHEAE

For online consultations, connect with Dr. Shiv Kumar Lath, a General Physician in Jharsuguda, on Lybrate: https://www.lybrate.com/jharsuguda/doctor/dr-shiv-kumar-lath-general-physician.

Stay connected with us through our various social media platforms and YouTube channel:

- Facebook Page: https://www.facebook.com/diabetesjharsuguda?mibextid=ZbWKwL

- Instagram: https://instagram.com/defeatdiabetesindia?igshid=MzNlNGNkZWQ4Mg==

- YouTube Channel: https://youtube.com/@patienteducation2101

To streamline your healthcare experience, download the HealthPlix app using this link: https://me-qr.com/m5BGzgPU

Share your feedback by rating us on JustDial: http://jsdl.in/JR-RTHQHH11786051.

Your engagement is important to us!

# CHAPTER ONE

# DEFINITION OF DIABETES MELLITUS

To understand diabetes mellitus, we must first understand insulin.

Insulin is a hormone, which is often referred to as a chemical. It is secreted by an organ called the pancreas, located in the upper part of our abdomen near our stomach. The pancreas secretes many chemicals that aid in the digestion of food, as well as several hormones that perform various functions in our body. Among these hormones, insulin is the most important one, responsible for controlling our blood sugar levels on a day-to-day basis.

When we eat food, it produces glucose in our body, and insulin regulates the glucose level. If our blood sugar rises above normal level, insulin secretion increases to lower it back down and vice versa. Insulin works by helping glucose molecules to enter inside.

However, if there is any disease or condition that decreases insulin secretion or quantity in our body (INSULIN DEFICIENCY), or prevents it from working correctly (INSULIN RESISTANCE) , it can cause our blood sugar level to fluctuate uncontrollably.

This condition is known as Diabetes Mellitus, and it results from defects in insulin secretion or action, or both.

Over time, uncontrolled blood sugar levels can lead to the failure of multiple organs, including the heart, kidneys, nerves, eyes, sexual functions, and other organs.

Therefore, it is essential to understand the role of insulin in our body and how it affects diabetes mellitus.

# CHAPTER TWO

# CLASSIFICATION

In our quest for understanding and managing diabetes, we classify it into two types for better clarity:

**1. Type 1 Diabetes:**

- A less common form.

- Caused by pancreatic beta cell destruction, leading to insulin deficiency.

- Treated solely with insulin due to its absolute deficiency.

**2. Type 2 Diabetes:**

- Predominantly due to insulin resistance.

- May or may not have partial insulin deficiency.

- Most common type; often manageable with medicines, and insulin isn't always required.

Beyond these, there are other types of diabetes due to factors like pancreas damage, hormonal imbalance, drug-induced causes, and gestational diabetes during pregnancy.

**For Patient Understanding:**

- The first two types are most crucial.

**Detailed Insights:**

**1. Type 1 Diabetes:**

- Lifelong insulin requirement for survival.

**2. Type 2 Diabetes:**

- Gradual onset, often after 30.

- Family history is common.
- Symptoms include weakness, weight loss, and genital infections.
- Responds to medicine; insulin is not always necessary.
**Important Note:**
- Don't try to diagnose the type of Diabetes Mellitus by yourself.
- The type of Diabetes is important from a Physician's point of view and you should not worry about that.
- -The major difference between the two is Insulin which is essential in Type 1 and not in Type 2 Diabetes Mellitus.
- A Serum C-peptide level and Fasting Serum Insulin level will differentiate between the two which will be on the lower side in Type 1 Diabetes Mellitus.

# CHAPTER THREE

# ETIOLOGY

Type 1 diabetes is due to absolute insulin deficiency, and the patient doesn't have any role in it.

Type 2 Diabetes Mellitus (T2DM) is a condition that can often be prevented or delayed through proactive lifestyle choices. As a patient, here are key steps you can take to reduce your risk and promote overall well-being.

**1. Maintain a Healthy Weight:**

Carrying excess weight, especially around the abdomen, increases the risk of developing diabetes. Adopt a balanced, portion-controlled diet and engage in regular physical activity to achieve and maintain a healthy weight.

**2. Make Wise Food Choices:**

Embrace a diet rich in fruits, vegetables, whole grains, and lean proteins. Limit the intake of processed foods, sugary snacks, and beverages. Opt for foods with a low glycemic index to help regulate blood sugar levels.

**3. Stay Active:**

Regular physical activity is a powerful tool in diabetes prevention. Aim for at least 150 minutes of moderate-intensity exercise per week, such as brisk walking, cycling, or swimming. Incorporate strength training exercises to enhance overall fitness.

**4. Monitor Blood Sugar Levels:**

If you are at risk of diabetes or have prediabetes, regularly monitor your blood sugar levels. Early detection allows for timely intervention and lifestyle adjustments to prevent progression to diabetes.

**5. Manage Stress:**

Chronic stress can contribute to unhealthy lifestyle choices. Practice stress-reducing techniques such as mindfulness, meditation, or deep breathing to promote emotional well-being.

**6. Get Adequate Sleep:**

Quality sleep is linked to better metabolic health. Aim for 7-9 hours of uninterrupted sleep each night to support overall health and reduce the risk of developing diabetes.

**7. Quit Smoking:**

Smoking is a significant risk factor for T2DM. If you smoke, seek support to quit. Quitting not only reduces diabetes risk but also improves overall health.

**8. Limit Alcohol Intake:**

Excessive alcohol consumption can contribute to weight gain and increase the risk of diabetes. If you choose to drink, do so in moderation—limiting intake to one drink per day for women and two drinks per day for men.

**9. Regular Check-ups:**

Attend regular check-ups with your healthcare provider. They can assess your diabetes risk, guide preventive measures, and monitor your overall health.

**10. Know Your Family History:**

Understand your family's health history, as genetics can play a role in diabetes risk. Be proactive in managing lifestyle factors if diabetes runs in your family.

By incorporating these lifestyle changes, you empower yourself to take control of your health and reduce the risk of developing Type 2 Diabetes Mellitus. Consult with your healthcare provider for personalized guidance and support on your diabetes prevention journey.

# CHAPTER FOUR

# DIAGNOSIS

When it comes to diagnosing diabetes, we rely on two key factors: symptoms and laboratory confirmation.
   - **Identifying Symptoms:**
   - Common symptoms include increased food intake (polyphagia), frequent urination (polyuria), and persistent thirst (polydipsia).
   - Additional indicators may include weight loss, urinary tract infections, issues during routine check ups, generalized weakness, pruritus,Unexplained body pain, etc

*"- **Laboratory Confirmation:**"*

- Various global criteria exist for diagnosis, but a straightforward method involves testing Fasting Plasma Glucose (FPG) and Random Plasma Glucose (RPG).
   - FPG levels above 126 mg/dL and RPG levels over 200 mg/dL, along with symptoms, indicate diabetes.
   - Confirmatory testing should be done on separate occasions and in different labs (NOT WITH GLUCOMETERS).

*"PRE-DIABETES"*

These are the patients who may develop Diabetes very soon so should take steps to prevent the development of full-blown Diabetes.

- **Diagnosis Criteria:**

- Fasting Plasma Glucose between 110 to 126 mg/dL indicates pre-diabetes.

- Impaired Glucose Tolerance (IGT) is diagnosed with a Postprandial Plasma Glucose level ranging from 140 to 200 mg/dL.

Any of the two criteria will diagnose a pre Diabetes case.

- **Preventive Measures:**

- This pre-diabetic stage is a warning, providing an opportunity to take preventive measures.

- Addressing pre-diabetes early may help avoid developing full-blown diabetes in the future.

Understanding these perspectives is pivotal in effectively managing diabetes. By adhering to medical recommendations, individuals can navigate diabetes, prevent complications, and lead a healthy life.

A NOTE ON GLUCOMETER

For individuals managing diabetes, a glucometer is a valuable tool for monitoring blood sugar levels at home. To ensure accurate readings and effective diabetes management, it's crucial to follow a set of dos and don'ts when using your glucometer.

**Dos:**

1. **Wash Your Hands:**

- DO wash your hands thoroughly with soap and water before testing. Residue on your fingers can affect the accuracy of the reading.

2. **Use Fresh Lancets:**

- DO use a new lancet for each test to ensure a clean and painless prick. Regularly change lancets to maintain their sharpness.

3. **Check Glucometer Accuracy:**

- DO regularly check the accuracy of your glucometer by comparing its readings with those obtained at your healthcare provider's office and always buy any 3 of the below-mentioned glucometers: Accu-check, Bayer Contour plus, One-Touch.

4. **Keep Test Strips Sealed:**

- DO keep your test strips in their original, sealed container. Exposure to air, moisture, or light can compromise their effectiveness.

5. **Calibrate Your Glucometer:**

- DO calibrate your glucometer as instructed by the manufacturer or your healthcare provider. Calibration ensures accurate readings.

6. **Follow Test Strip Storage Instructions:**

- DO store your test strips according to the manufacturer's instructions. Improper storage can lead to inaccurate results.

7. **Code Your Meter Correctly:**

- DO code your glucometer with the correct code corresponding to the batch of test strips you are using. Incorrect coding can lead to inaccurate readings.

8. **Keep a Log of Readings:**

- DO maintain a log of your blood sugar readings, along with notes on factors that may influence them, such as meals, exercise, and medication.

**Don'ts:**

1. **Use Expired Test Strips:**

- DON'T use expired test strips. Expired strips may provide inaccurate readings, compromising the effectiveness of your diabetes management.

2. **Squeeze Your Finger Too Hard:**

- DON'T squeeze your finger too hard when obtaining a blood sample. Squeezing can alter the composition of the blood, leading to inaccurate results.

3. **Neglect Regular Metre Cleaning:**

- DON'T neglect cleaning your glucometer regularly. A clean metre ensures accurate readings and prevents contamination.

4. **Skip Quality Control Checks:**

- DON'T skip routine quality control checks recommended by the manufacturer. These checks help ensure the reliability of your glucometer.

5. **Reuse Lancets:**

- DON'T reuse lancets. While it may seem convenient, using a new lancet for each test minimises pain and reduces the risk of infection.

6. **Ignore Environmental Conditions:**

- DON'T expose your glucometer to extreme temperatures, humidity, or direct sunlight. Protect it from environmental conditions that may affect its performance.

7. **Overlook Battery Levels:**

- DON'T overlook the battery level of your glucometer. Low battery levels can result in inaccurate readings.

By adhering to these dos and don'ts, you can maximise the accuracy of your glucometer readings, empowering yourself to make informed decisions about your diabetes management. Always consult with your healthcare provider for personalised guidance on blood sugar monitoring and diabetes care.

# CHAPTER FIVE

# SCREENING OF DIABETES

Screening for diabetes in normal or high-risk groups is crucial for early diagnosis when a patient is asymptomatic, as a delayed diagnosis can result in significant organ damage.

The following individuals should undergo diabetes screening at home:

- Individuals with a BMI exceeding 25 kg per square metre.

- Patients who are physically inactive or sedentary.

- First-degree relatives of patients with diabetes mellitus.

- Women who delivered a baby weighing more than 4 kg in their last delivery.

- Individuals with a history of high blood pressure.

- Presence of triglyceride levels exceeding 250 milligrams per deciliter.

- Women who were diagnosed with polycystic ovary syndrome in the past.

- Patients previously diagnosed with gestational diabetes.

- Individuals with a history of cardiovascular disease, such as heart attack, angina, or blockages in the heart.

In layman's terms, if any of the above factors are present in an individual, diabetes screening should be initiated every 6 months. Additionally:

- Screening should commence for individuals after the age of 35.

- If the initial screening is normal, subsequent screenings should be conducted every 3 to 4 years according to conventional guidelines.

- However, in my opinion, annual screenings are more prudent, considering the unpredictable nature of blood sugar fluctuations and the potential onset of diabetes mellitus.

CHAPTER SIX

# MANAGEMENT

When managing a diabetes case, several steps must be taken. The primary focus is on lifestyle modification, encompassing two fundamental aspects: diet and exercise. Let's delve into each aspect individually.

**AFTER THAT WE WILL DISCUSS ON DIFFERENT MEDICINES AVAILABLE FOR TREATMENT OF DIABETES**

**Diet:**

- It's important to note that a fixed diet chart is often impractical for a lifetime. Instead, understanding the basics of creating a personalised dietary pattern is key to controlling blood sugar levels effectively.

- Patients frequently request diet charts, but it's crucial to acknowledge that the advice provided here is not a substitute for a diet chart from a qualified dietitian. Many patients in India lack access to proper dietitians, prompting the need for practical advice.

- With the availability of the Internet and online dietitians, patients can now control their blood sugar levels more effectively. Various mobile applications also offer assistance in maintaining blood sugar within a normal range.

- To create a diet chart, the first step is to estimate the patient's calorie requirement, depending on their overall nutritional status and activity level. Two methods are available: manual and computerised.

- The computerised method involves searching Google for the calorie requirement, providing an exact figure after entering valid data.

- The manual method requires calculating the ideal body weight using the formula: (height in centimetres - 100) * 0.9.

- The recommended daily calorie intake varies based on factors such as weight, age, and pregnancy status. For example:

- Normal weight: 30 kilocalories per kg

- Overweight: 20 kilocalories per kg

- Underweight: 40 kilocalories per kg

- After the age of 50, reduce the calculated calorie by 10%.

- The total calorie requirement is then divided into different types of food, such as carbohydrates, proteins, and fats. A suggested distribution is 60% for carbohydrates and 20% each for proteins and fats.

- Before creating a personal diet chart, make a list of common foods consumed over 5 to 7 days. Categorise them based on their main components (carbohydrates, proteins, fats), calculate the calorie content, and determine the serving size according to daily requirements.

- In situations where unfamiliar foods are introduced or during emergencies, it's crucial to calculate the calorie content using online resources or food packaging to maintain stable blood sugar levels.

This provides a rough idea of how to create a personalised diet chart. Now, let's explore common foods to be avoided by individuals with diabetes.

**Carbohydrates:**

- Avoid all kinds of sweets, including sugar, jaggery, honey, sweets made from maida, suji, and underground food items.

- Refrain from consuming white rice, especially polished white rice.

- Instead, opt for whole wheat, brown rice, dal, green vegetables, and salads.

*Explanation of Glycemic Index:*

Before moving forward, it's crucial to understand the concept of Glycemic Index (GI):

- GI represents the density of calories present in a food item.

- For example, a small gulab jamun may contain approximately 300 calories, but its impact on blood sugar is disproportionate. Consuming 2 to 3 gulab jamuns, along with other snacks, can result in a rapid spike in blood sugar within a short duration.

- In contrast, a balanced meal with two chapatis, dal, yogurt, green vegetables, etc., provides the same calorie intake but sustains it over 6 to 7 hours. This is due to the lower glycemic index of the entire meal.

- High glycemic index foods, like gulab jamun, cause a rapid increase in blood sugar levels, whereas a well-balanced thali has a slower impact, promoting a feeling of fullness.

**List of Low Glycemic Index Foods:**

Include the following in your diet:

- Whole grains
- Legumes
- Beans
- Lentils

- Almonds
- Walnuts
- Flaxseeds
- Various fruits such as berries, cherries, etc.
- Vegetables like broccoli, cauliflower, spinach, leafy green vegetables, etc.

**Fats:**

- All fats should be consumed in moderation, constituting only 20% of the daily calorie intake.

- The maximum fat or oil intake should be *500 ml per person per month* in a family.

- Ideally, use a mix of different oils, changing them monthly. Avoid using a single oil throughout the year.

- Steer clear of ghee, butter, Vanaspati, palm oil, coconut oil, and extra oils for cooking.

- Choose healthier options like *rice bran oil, mustard oil, sesame oil, sunflower oil, olive oil, canola oil, and gingelly oil,* as they contain polyunsaturated fatty acids.

**Proteins:**

- Protein is a crucial food item for the growth and maintenance of body cells, constituting 20% of the total calorie intake.

- The daily requirement is one gram per day per kilogram of body weight.

- *Even kidney disease patients should consume at least 0.8 grams of protein per day* to prevent malnutrition.

- Vegetable proteins like milk ,dal,soyabeans and paneer are preferable to non-vegetarian proteins.

- In non-vegetarian options, fish and lean meat are better than processed meat.

- High animal protein should be avoided in any case.

**Fibres:**

- Fibres are foods that are not absorbed in the intestinal tract, causing no rise in blood sugar levels.

- They pass unabsorbed in the stool, increasing stool bulk and preventing constipation.

- Foods high in fibre include whole grain cereals, leafy vegetables, and colourful vegetables like barley.

**Alcohol:**

- Alcohol should be avoided by all patients, as it increases the risk of heart and lung diseases, as well as stomach and lung cancers.

- Smoking should be stopped to reduce the risk of complications in diabetes mellitus, such as coronary artery disease and paralysis.

**Fruits for diabetes patients:**

Patient can take:

1.    **Berries   (e.g.,   Blueberries,   Strawberries, Raspberries):**

2. **Apples:** Contain fibre and have a moderate glycemic index.

3. **Cherries:** Despite containing natural sugars, they have anti-inflammatory properties.

4. **Pears:** High in fibre and relatively low in natural sugars.

5. **Peaches:** Provide vitamins and fibre with a moderate impact on blood sugar.

6. **Plums:** Rich in antioxidants and fibre, with a lower glycemic index.

7. **Kiwi:** Packed with nutrients, including fibre and vitamin C.

8. **Guava:** Contains dietary fibre and is relatively low in sugar.

9. **Avocado:** While technically a fruit, it's low in sugar and high in healthy fats.

*Should avoid fruits like:*

1. Pineapple

2. Ripe Bananas

3. Mangoes

4. Grapes

5.Watermelon

- **Always avoid consumption of fruit juices**

- **Always avoid consumption of Juicy and ripe fruits.**

**Exercise:**

Certainly! Regular exercise offers a multitude of benefits for everyone, regardless of age or fitness level. Here are some key advantages:

1. **Improved Cardiovascular Health**: Exercise strengthens the heart and improves circulation, reducing the risk of heart disease.

2. **Weight Management**: Regular physical activity helps in maintaining a healthy weight by burning calories and boosting metabolism.

3. **Muscle Strength and Flexibility**: Exercise enhances muscle strength, endurance, and flexibility, contributing to overall physical fitness.

4. **Better Mental Health**: Physical activity releases endorphins, reducing stress and anxiety while improving mood and cognitive function.

5. **Bone Health**: Weight-bearing exercises contribute to bone density, reducing the risk of osteoporosis and fractures.

6. **Enhanced Sleep Quality**: Regular exercise promotes better sleep patterns, leading to improved overall sleep quality.

7. **Increased Energy Levels**: Physical activity improves endurance and energy levels, making daily tasks

easier to perform.

8. **Improved Immune System**: Regular exercise can boost the immune system, reducing the risk of illness and promoting overall health.

9. **Better Posture and Balance**: Strength training and core exercises contribute to improved posture and balance, reducing the risk of falls and injuries.

10. **Social Connection**: Group exercises or team sports provide opportunities for social interaction, fostering a sense of community and support.

11. **Reduced Risk of Chronic Diseases**: Regular physical activity lowers the risk of various chronic conditions, including diabetes, hypertension, and certain cancers.

12. **Enhanced Cognitive Function**: Exercise has been linked to improved cognitive function, including better memory and attention span.

13. **Health Boost: Balanced Blood Pressure and Cholesterol**

14. **Diabetes Defence: Enhanced Insulin Sensitivity**
- Improve insulin sensitivity.
- Reduce the risk of early insulin use.

Select activities you love for a sustainable and enjoyable exercise routine. We suggest trying YouTube workout videos at home for a bite-free, weather-independent, comfortable, and cost-effective option.

*Exercising with diabetes requires some considerations. Here are some recommendations and precautions:*

1. **Consult with a healthcare professional:** Before starting any exercise program, it's crucial to consult with your healthcare team. They can provide personalised advice based on your individual health status.

2. **Choose the right type of exercise:** Aim for a mix of aerobic exercises (like walking, swimming, or cycling) ,stretching and strength training. This combination helps improve insulin sensitivity and overall health.

3. **Regularity is key:** Consistency is more important than intensity. Aim for at least 150 minutes of moderate-intensity aerobic exercise per week, along with strength training exercises at least two days a week. start with warm up for 10-15 minutes

4. **Monitor blood sugar levels:** Regularly check your blood sugar levels before, during, and after exercise. This helps you understand how your body responds to different activities and adjust accordingly.

5. **Stay hydrated:** Dehydration can affect blood sugar levels. Drink plenty of water before, during, and after exercise.

6. **Carry a snack:** Always have a fast-acting carbohydrate snack on hand, such as glucose tablets or a small juice box, in case your blood sugar drops during exercise, especially if you already have kidney disease or history of frequent hypoglycemia.

**Precautions:**

1. **Temperature Caution:** Extreme heat or cold can impact blood sugar levels. Take steps to regulate your body temperature in such conditions.

2. **Foot Check:** Due to diabetes, your feet ' nerves can be affected. Before and after exercise, inspect for cuts or sores. Wear proper footwear to prevent injuries.

3. **Hypoglycemia Awareness:** Exercise may lead to low blood sugar. Recognize symptoms and have a fast-acting carbohydrate on hand for prompt treatment.

4. **Meal Consistency:** Don't skip meals; maintain balanced eating before exercising to avoid blood sugar

fluctuations.

5. **Adapt Activities:** If complications like retinopathy or neuropathy exist, modify or avoid certain exercises. Listen to your body and adjust accordingly.

6. **Foot Protection:** Avoid walking barefoot; use quality shoes during exercise to prevent foot damage and potential ulcers.

7. **ID Card Essential:** Carry an ID card with your details for emergencies outside, aiding in situations like hypoglycemia, chest pain, or stroke.

8. **Chest Pain Alert:** Cease exercise if chest pain develops.

*Sometimes life gets so hectic that dedicating time to a workout seems impossible. But fear not, there are alternatives to traditional exercise that can be seamlessly integrated into a busy schedule:*

1. **Incorporate movement into daily tasks:**
- Take the stairs instead of the elevator.
- Park farther away to get in some extra steps.
- Do squats or calf raises while brushing your teeth.
2. **Desk exercises:**
- Do seated leg lifts or knee extensions under your desk.
- Incorporate seated torso twists.
- Stretch your neck and shoulders periodically.
3. **Short bursts of activity:**
- Break your day into small segments. Take a 5-minute break every hour to stretch or walk.
- Try high-intensity interval training (HIIT) with quick, intense bursts of activity.
4. **Active commuting:**
- If possible, walk or bike to work.
- If you use public transportation, get off at a stop earlier and walk the rest of the way.

5. **Micro-workouts:**
- Fit in quick exercises throughout the day, like 5 minutes of jumping jacks, push-ups, or squats.
6. **Dance it out:**
- Dance while doing household chores or during a break. It's a fun way to get your heart rate up.
7. **Stretching routines:**
- Incorporate stretching exercises into your morning or bedtime routine. It can improve flexibility and relaxation.
8. **Use technology:**
- Try fitness apps that offer short, effective workouts.
- Set reminders on your phone to stand up, stretch, or take a quick walk.
9. **Active meetings:**
- Propose walking meetings or stand while on conference calls.
10. **Prioritise sleep:**
- While not a direct substitute for exercise, ensuring you get enough sleep is crucial for overall health and can impact your energy levels.

**Yoga**

Here are a few yoga poses that may be helpful for individuals with type 2 diabetes:

1. **Child's Pose (Balasana):** This pose helps to relax the mind and lower stress levels.

2. **Downward-Facing Dog (Adho Mukha Svanasana):** This pose stretches and strengthens the entire body, improving circulation.

3. **Seated Forward Bend (Paschimottanasana):** Helps stimulate the liver and kidneys, which can be beneficial for diabetes management.

4. **Bridge Pose (Setu Bandhasana):** Strengthens the legs and stimulates the thyroid gland, which may help

regulate metabolism.

5. **Legs Up the Wall Pose (Viparita Karani):** This restorative pose can help reduce stress and improve circulation.

6. **Twisting Poses (e.g., Seated Twist or Bharadvajasana):** Twisting poses may help massage the organs, including the pancreas.

Remember to start slowly, listen to your body, and avoid overexertion. Consistency is key, and it's crucial to combine yoga with a balanced diet and other forms of exercise as part of an overall diabetes management plan. Always consult with your healthcare provider before making significant changes to your routine.

**Stress Management:**

Managing stress and anxiety is crucial for maintaining overall well-being. Here are some strategies you might find helpful:

1. **Deep Breathing:** Practise deep, diaphragmatic breathing. Inhale slowly through your nose, hold for a few seconds, and exhale slowly through your mouth. This can help activate your body's relaxation response.

2. **Mindfulness Meditation:** Engage in mindfulness or meditation practices. These techniques can help you stay present and calm your mind.

3. **Regular Exercise:** Physical activity is a great stress reliever. It helps release endorphins, which are natural mood lifters.

4. **Healthy Lifestyle:** Ensure you're getting enough sleep, maintaining a balanced diet, and staying hydrated. These factors can significantly impact your stress levels.

5. **Set Realistic Goals:** Break down tasks into smaller, more manageable parts. Celebrate your achievements, no matter how small, and don't be too hard on yourself.

6. **Social Support:** Share your feelings with someone you trust. Talking about what's stressing you can be therapeutic, and supportive friends or family can provide valuable perspectives.

7. **Time Management:** Prioritise your tasks and tackle them one at a time. Avoid overloading yourself with too many responsibilities.

8. **Limit Stimulants:** Reduce your intake of caffeine and other stimulants, especially in the hours leading up to bedtime.

9. **Learn to Say No:** It's okay to decline additional responsibilities if you feel overwhelmed. Setting boundaries is crucial for managing stress.

10. **Seek Professional Help:** If your stress and anxiety persist, consider seeking help from a mental health professional. They can provide guidance and support tailored to your specific situation.

Remember, it's okay to ask for help, and taking small steps consistently can make a big difference over time. What strategies do you find most helpful? Please mail me in my mail ID later on.

**MEDICINES**

Let's dive into the two main types of treatments for diabetes: medicines, also known as oral hypoglycemic agents, and insulin, administered through injections. I'll guide you through a comprehensive understanding of diabetes medications, breaking them down into different groups. Within each group, I'll detail the commonly used medicines for diabetes treatment, including their brand names.

Here's a helpful breakdown:

- **Understanding Medicines:**

- Explore the various groups of medicines used for diabetes treatment.

- Learn about common brand names associated with each medicine group.

- **Matching Brands:**

- Match the brand names mentioned here with the composition on your medicine strip.

- This will help you identify the specific medicine you're using.

- **Global Varieties:**

- Keep in mind that there are numerous brands available in India and worldwide.

- If you can't find details about your specific medicine in this guide, simply search the medicine name on Google to discover its compound name.

By following these steps, you'll be equipped with the knowledge to understand and manage the medicines you're taking for diabetes.

**METFORMIN:**

Metformin is a widely prescribed medication for managing type 2 diabetes.

**Common Brand Names:**

- Glycomet

- Metfor

- Glyciphage

**How to Take Metformin:**

- Take Metformin as prescribed by your healthcare provider.

- Commonly *administered with meals* to mitigate gastrointestinal side effects.

- Adhere to the recommended dosage and schedule for optimal effectiveness.

**Side Effects:**

Metformin is generally well-tolerated, but some individuals may experience the following common side effects, especially during the initial stages of treatment. It's essential to inform your healthcare provider if these effects persist or worsen over time:

1. **Nausea:** Feeling queasy or experiencing an urge to vomit.

2. **Diarrhoea:** Loose or watery stools.

3. **Stomach Upset:** Discomfort or irritation in the stomach.

These side effects are often temporary and tend to subside as the body adjusts to the medication. It's crucial to maintain open communication with your healthcare provider to address any concerns and ensure the appropriate management of side effects.

In case of severe or persistent side effects, seek prompt medical attention. It's important to follow your healthcare provider's guidance for a consistent and effective treatment plan. Remember, this information is not exhaustive, and individual responses may vary. Always consult with your healthcare professional for personalized advice tailored to your health needs.

**SULFONYLUREA**

**Different Compounds:**

1. **Glibenclamide (Glyburide):**

- One of the oldest and most commonly prescribed sulfonylureas.

- Usually taken once or twice a day with meals.

2. **Gliclazide:**

- A newer sulfonylurea with a shorter half-life.

- Typically taken once or twice a day with meals.

3. **Glimepiride:**

- Known for its longer duration of action compared to other sulfonylureas.
- Usually taken once daily, often with breakfast.
**Popular Brand Names in India and Overseas:**
1. **Glibenclamide (Glyburide):**
- Micronase (Overseas)
- Daonil (India)
2. **Gliclazide:**
- Diamicron (Overseas)
- Diamicron MR (India)
3. **Glimepiride:**
- Amaryl (Overseas)
- Glimy (India)
- Isryl (India)
**Side Effects:**
While generally well-tolerated, sulfonylureas may have side effects, including:
1. **Hypoglycemia:** Low blood sugar, especially if meals are skipped or if the dosage is too high,So always take it before taking measles or food only.
2. **Weight Gain:** Some individuals may experience weight gain.
3. **Gastrointestinal Upset:** Nausea or stomach discomfort.
**Dos:**
1. **Take with Meals:** To reduce the risk of hypoglycemia, take sulfonylureas just before meals.
2. **Regular Monitoring:** Keep track of blood sugar levels and attend regular check-ups.
**Don'ts:**
1. **Skip Meals:** Maintain a consistent meal schedule to support medication effectiveness.

2. **Consume Excessive Alcohol:** Limit alcohol intake, as it can increase the risk of hypoglycemia.

**4.REPAGLINIDE :**

Is a short-acting sulfonylurea-like used to control *Postprandial Hyperglycemia* in some patients.

**Common Brands in India:**

Repaglinide is available under various brand names in India, including Novonorm, Repilin, and Eurepa, among others.

**Dose:**

. It is typically taken before meals, usually 15-30 minutes before each main meal. The specific dose will be determined by your healthcare provider.

**Adverse Effects:**

Common side effects of Repaglinide include hypoglycemia (low blood sugar), weight gain, and gastrointestinal issues such as nausea or stomach upset .

It's important to monitor blood sugar levels 4 times while taking this class of medicines Before B/F,After B/F,Lunch and Dinner too and report to your doctor.

**THIAZONIDINE DIONE:**

Only 1 molecule is being used now a dayswhich is Pioglitazone.

PIOGLITAZONE:

**Common Brands in India:**

Pioglitazone is available under various brand names in India, including *Pioz, P-Glitz, Piosys and Glizone*, among others.

**Dose:**

The dosage of Pioglitazone can vary based on individual factors such as the patient's response to the medication and the overall management of diabetes.The most widely used is 15 g.

Commonly, it is taken once daily, with or without meals.
**How to Take:**
Pioglitazone is typically taken orally with a full glass of water.

The medication can be taken with or without food, but consistency in timing is important for effectiveness.*It should be taken at same time everyday.*

**Adverse Effects:**

Common side effects of Pioglitazone include weight gain, edema (fluid retention leading to swelling), and an increased risk of fractures, especially in women. Pioglitazone may also affect liver function, so regular monitoring is often recommended.

**ALPHA GLUCOSIDASE INHIBITOR:**

2 COMPOUNDS ARE AVAILABLE UNDER THIS GROUP OF DRUGS:

1.ACARBOSE

2.VOGLIBOSE

Let us discuss one by one

**1.ACARBOSE:**

**Common Brands in India:**

Acarbose is available in India under various brand names, including *Glucobay and Gluformin.*

**How to Take:**

Acarbose is usually taken orally with water, and it's important to take the medication with the first bite of each main meal. The timing is crucial as Acarbose works by slowing the digestion of carbohydrates in the intestines, helping to control postprandial (after-meal) blood sugar levels.

**Adverse Effects:**

Common side effects of Acarbose include gastrointestinal issues such as *flatulence, diarrhoea, and abdominal discomfort*. These side effects are often transient and may improve over time. Starting with a low dose and gradually increasing it can help minimise these effects. Hypoglycemia (low blood sugar) is less likely to occur with Acarbose alone, but it may occur if taken in combination with other diabetes medications.

**2.VOGLIBOSE:**

**Common Brands in India:**

Voglibose is available in India under various brand names, including *Vogs,Megavog,Vogli etc*

**How to Take:**

Voglibose is usually taken orally with water, and it's *important to take the medication with meals* to help control postprandial (after-meal) blood sugar levels.

**Adverse Effects:**

Common side effects of Voglibose include gastrointestinal issues such as flatulence, diarrhea, and abdominal discomfort. These side effects are often transient and may improve over time.

**INCRETIN BASED THERAPY:**

We have 2 class of drugs under this group:

1.GLP 1 analogues

2.DPP 4 inhibitors

Let us discuss one by one:

**GLP-1 ANALOGS:**

**Introduction:**

Glucagon-like peptide-1 (GLP-1) analogs are a class of medications designed to help manage blood sugar levels in individuals with type 2 diabetes. This article provides a brief overview of the different compounds, popular brand names available in India and overseas, potential side effects, and essential dos and don'ts when using GLP-1 analogs.

**Different Compounds:**

1. **Exenatide:**
- A synthetic form of the hormone GLP-1.
- Available as immediate-release (Byetta) and extended-release (Bydureon) formulations.
2. **Liraglutide:**
- A once-daily injectable GLP-1 analog.
- Sold under the brand name Victoza.
3. **Dulaglutide:**
- Administered once weekly.
- Available under the brand name Trulicity.
4. **Semaglutide:**
- Comes in both once-weekly and oral tablet formulations.
- Branded as Ozempic (injection) and Rybelsus (oral).
**Side Effects:**
While generally well-tolerated, GLP-1 analogs may have side effects, including:
1. **Nausea:** Especially during initial use, but often diminishes over time.
2. **Diarrhoea:** May occur but tends to be transient.
3. **Injection Site Reactions:** Common with injectable formulations.
4. **Hypoglycemia:** Risk is lower compared to some other diabetes medications.
**2.DPP 4 INHIBITORS:**
Dipeptidyl peptidase-4 (DPP-4) inhibitors are a class of medications used in the management of type 2 diabetes. Here's an overview of patient information, including common brands in India, dosage, administration, adverse effects, and contraindications:
**Common DPP-4 Inhibitors in India:**
1. **Sitagliptin:**
- Common Brands: Januvia, Istavel, Sitamet

- Dosage: The usual dose is 100 mg once daily, with or without food. Dosage adjustments may be made based on kidney function.

**2. **Vildagliptin:****

- Common Brands: Galvus, Jalra, Vysov,Vildamac

- Dosage: The typical dose is 50 mg twice daily. Adjustments may be made based on kidney function. Now a sustained-release formulation is available in 100-gram doses which can be taken once daily like Jalra OD.

- Administration: Vildagliptin is usually taken orally with or without food.

**3. **Saxagliptin:****

- Common Brands: Onglyza, Zomelis

- Dosage: The standard dose is 2.5 mg or 5 mg once daily, with or without food. Adjustments may be necessary for kidney function.

- Administration: Saxagliptin is taken orally.

**4. **Linagliptin:****

- Common Brands:

- Linamet,Linero,Ondero

- Dosage: The usual dose is 5 mg once daily. *No dosage adjustments are typically needed for kidney function.*

**5. **Teneligliptin:****

- **Common Brands in India:**

-Tenglyn

-Teneligliptin

-Dynaglipt

- **Dosage:**

- The typical dose for teneligliptin is 20 mg once daily.

- **Administration:**

- Teneligliptin is taken orally with or without food

**Adverse Effects:**

Common adverse effects for DPP-4 inhibitors may include upper respiratory tract infections, headache, and gastrointestinal symptoms such as nausea or diarrhoea.

Severe side effects are rare but may include pancreatitis.

**SGLT-2 inhibitors:**

**Advantages of SGLT-2 Inhibitors:**

1. **Glucose Lowering:** SGLT-2 inhibitors help lower blood glucose levels by inhibiting the reabsorption of glucose in the kidneys, leading to increased glucose excretion in the urine.

2. **Weight Loss:** Some individuals may experience weight loss with SGLT-2 inhibitors, which can be beneficial for those with overweight or obesity.

3. **Blood Pressure Reduction:** SGLT-2 inhibitors have been associated with a mild reduction in blood pressure, which can be advantageous for individuals with hypertension.

4. **Cardiovascular Benefits:** Certain SGLT-2 inhibitors have shown cardiovascular benefits, including a reduction in the risk of cardiovascular events and heart failure hospitalisation.

5. **Renal Protection:** SGLT-2 inhibitors may offer renal protection by slowing the progression of kidney disease in some individuals with diabetes.

**Disadvantages of SGLT-2 Inhibitors:**

1. **Genital and Urinary Tract Infections:** SGLT-2 inhibitors are associated with an increased risk of genital yeast infections and urinary tract infections.

2. **Polyuria and Thirst:** Increased glucose excretion in the urine can lead to more frequent urination (polyuria) and increased thirst.

3. **Dehydration:** SGLT-2 inhibitors can contribute to dehydration, especially in older adults or those taking

diuretics

**Common SGLT-2 Inhibitors in India:**

1. **Empagliflozin:**

- Common Brands: Jardiance, Glyxambi, Ajaduo

- Dosage: The usual dose is 10 mg or 25 mg once daily in the morning, with or without food. Adjustments may be made based on kidney function.

2. **Dapagliflozin:**

- Common Brands: Dapamac,Damita,Forxiga etc

- Dosage: The typical dose is 5 mg or 10 mg once daily, with or without food. Adjustments may be needed based on kidney function.

3. **Canagliflozin:**

- Common Brands: Invokana, Canapril, Cantiflo,Sulisent

- Dosage: The usual dose is 100 mg or 300 mg once daily, with or without food. Adjustments may be made based on kidney function.

- Administration: Canagliflozin is taken orally.

Stay well-hydrated by drinking plenty of water when taking this category of medications.


**IMEGLIMIN:**

imeglimin is a novel investigational medication for the treatment of type 2 diabetes. It's essential to note that the status and availability of drugs can change, and new information may have emerged since then.

Here are the potential advantages and disadvantages associated with imeglimin:

**Advantages:**

1. **Unique Mechanism of Action:** Imeglimin works through a novel mechanism of action by targeting mitochondrial bioenergetics and improving insulin

sensitivity. It is the first in a new class of oral antidiabetic agents known as tetrahydro triazines.

2. **Blood Glucose Control:** Imeglimin has shown promise in improving glycemic control by reducing fasting and postprandial glucose levels.

3. **Low Risk of Hypoglycemia:** Imeglimin is believed to have a low risk of causing hypoglycemia (low blood sugar) when used as a monotherapy.

4. **Weight-Neutral or Weight-Loss Effects:** Some early studies suggested that imeglimin may be weight-neutral or associated with weight loss, which can be beneficial for individuals with overweight or obesity.

Given that imeglimin is a relatively new player in the field of antidiabetic medications, ongoing research and clinical trials are needed to further elucidate its benefits, risks, and long-term effects.

Note:

There are some misconceptions related to Medicines used for Diabetes in India, here is a note to remove those misconceptions.

It's understandable to think that a higher milligram (mg) dosage means a stronger or more potent medication. However, in the world of medicine, things aren't always that straightforward. I'd like to shed some light on this matter, using the example of glimepiride and metformin.

Glimepiride, at a dose of 2 mg, may seem lower in milligrams compared to metformin at 500 mg, but it's crucial to understand that the efficacy and mechanism of action of these medications differ. Glimepiride belongs to a class of drugs known as sulfonylureas, which stimulate the pancreas to produce more insulin. On the other hand, metformin, a biguanide, works by reducing glucose production in the liver and improving insulin sensitivity in the body.

In simpler terms, comparing the mg dosage directly might not accurately reflect the strength or effectiveness of these medications. Glimepiride, at 2 mg, can have a more potent impact on blood sugar control than metformin at 500 mg, despite the apparent difference in dosage.

**INSULIN**

There are many myths associated with Insulin let us first try to debunk them one by one

**Myth 1: Insulin is only for people with severe diabetes.**

- **Explanation:** Insulin is a treatment option for various types and stages of diabetes. It's not just for severe cases; many people with diabetes, both Type 1 and Type 2, may use insulin to manage their blood sugar levels at different points in their treatment.

**Myth 2: Insulin is the last resort; oral medications are always enough.**

- **Explanation:** While oral medications are common for managing diabetes, insulin may be necessary when these medications are no longer effective or when more intensive glucose control is needed.

**Myth 3: Insulin causes weight gain.**

- **Explanation:** While some people may experience weight gain with insulin, it's not a universal effect. Proper diet and lifestyle choices, along with insulin adjustments, can help manage weight. The primary goal of insulin is to regulate blood sugar levels.

**Myth 4: Insulin injections are extremely painful.**

- **Explanation:** Modern insulin needles are very thin, and the injection process is usually not very painful. Many people find the discomfort minimal, especially with proper injection techniques. The benefits of insulin in managing diabetes often outweigh any temporary discomfort.

**Myth 5: Insulin is only for old people with diabetes.**

- **Explanation:** Diabetes and the need for insulin can affect people of all ages, including children and young adults. The necessity for insulin depends on the type and progression of diabetes, not just age.

**Myth 6: Once you start insulin, you can't stop it later.**

- **Explanation:** In some cases, insulin may be a temporary part of diabetes management, but for many, it becomes a long-term or lifelong requirement. The need for insulin depends on the individual's response to treatment, and stopping it without proper guidance can lead to uncontrolled blood sugar levels.

**Myth 7: Insulin causes low blood sugar (hypoglycemia) all the time.**

- **Explanation:** While insulin can lead to hypoglycemia if not used correctly, proper dosing and monitoring can minimise this risk. The goal is to find the right balance to maintain stable blood sugar levels.

**Myth 8: Insulin is addictive.**

- **Explanation:** Insulin is not addictive. It is a necessary treatment for managing diabetes, and individuals use it under the guidance of healthcare professionals to maintain healthy blood sugar levels.

**Myth 9: Insulin given means sugar treated.

_** Explanation:** Patients taking insulin need more stringent blood sugar check up and regular follow up to determine the exact dosage needed for you, and that dosage is more important than mere taking insulin only.

Effective management of insulin plays a pivotal role in keeping blood sugar levels in check, emphasising the need for regular communication between patients and their physicians. The frequency of these check-ins hinges on how well blood sugar is being regulated. To streamline this process, our clinic has instituted a comprehensive blood sugar control system.

Here's a breakdown of our approach:

- **Check-In Frequency:**

- The frequency of physician visits depends on blood sugar control.

- A personalised approach is tailored to individual observations.

- **Blood Sugar Monitoring Day:**

- On the designated day, patients monitor blood sugar four times:

- Before breakfast

- 2 hours after breakfast

- 2 hours after lunch

- 2 hours after dinner

- **Reporting Process:**

- Patients submit their reports via WhatsApp, including:

- Name

- Details

- Type of insulin in use

- pregnant or not

- **Adjusting Insulin Dosage:**

- Based on blood sugar levels, insulin dosage may be adjusted from our side via whatsapp

- This personalised fine-tuning helps bring blood sugar under control in a matter of days or weeks.

- **Universal Applicability:**

- This structured protocol is applicable to both diabetes and gestational diabetes patients.

By implementing this systematic blood sugar control system, we aim to empower our patients to actively participate in managing their health and achieving optimal blood sugar levels.

It's essential for patients to follow this routine diligently. Those who neglect this exercise may struggle to control their blood sugar levels, experiencing persistently high readings despite their commitment to daily insulin intake. Regular communication and adherence to this system are vital for effective diabetes management.

With these explanations I hope I am able to solve all questions in your mind ,still if you have doubts you can contact me at drsklath@gmail.com

Remember Precision in insulin dosage is crucial for stable blood sugar levels and a better quality of life. It's not just about taking insulin; it's about taking the right amount for personalised control.

**INDICATIONS OF INSULIN**

Insulin is a hormone that plays a crucial role in regulating blood sugar levels. In diabetes, the body either does not produce enough insulin (Type 1 diabetes) or does not use insulin effectively (Type 2 diabetes). Insulin therapy is prescribed for diabetes patients in various situations to help manage blood sugar levels. Here are some common indications for giving insulin in diabetes:

1. **Type 1 Diabetes:**

2. **Type 2 Diabetes:**

- **Insulin Resistance:** For some individuals with Type 2 diabetes, especially when oral medications or other injectable medications are not sufficient to control blood sugar levels due to insulin resistance.

4. **Gestational Diabetes:**

5. **Surgery and Hospitalisation:**

6. **High HbA1c Levels:**

7. **Sick Days:**

Some patients resist taking insulin due to various concerns. However, we provide insulin whenever it is deemed necessary, considering individual circumstances as mentioned above.

**TYPES OF INSULIN**

Insulin can be divided broadly into

1.Conventional Insulin

Which further is of 2 types according to the delivery system:

a.Vials

b.Insulin pens

2.Insulin Analogs

1.CONVENTIONAL INSULINS(VIALS)

Here are some common types of insulin vials marketed in India, excluding insulin analogs:

1. **Regular (Short-acting) Insulin Vials:**

- Human Actrapid

- Lupisulin R

2. **Intermediate-acting Insulin Vials:**

- **Humulin N (NPH)**

- **Novolin N (NPH)**

3. **Long-acting Insulin Vials:**

- **Lantus (Glargine)**

- **Basaglar (Glargine)**

- **Toujeo (Glargine)**

4. **Mixed Insulin Vials (Combination of Short-acting and Intermediate-acting):**

- **Human Mixtard 30/70 (Mix of NPH and Regular)**

These insulin vials are traditional, non-analog options that have been used for many years to help manage blood sugar levels in individuals with diabetes.

Note: But out of all these options Regular and MIxtard 30/70 Insulins are important and we use these types of

Insulin only as they are pocket-friendly and easily available.

The list given above is only for education purpose and the type of Insulin patient needs depends on choice of Doctor prescribing you the Insulin

INSULIN PENS (CONVENTIONAL INSULIN)

Insulin pens offer several advantages for people managing diabetes. Here are some key benefits:

1. **Convenience:**

- *Advantage:* Insulin pens are portable and easy to use, making them convenient for people who need to take insulin injections on the go.

2. **Accuracy:**

- *Advantage:* Insulin pens provide a more precise dose compared to vials and syringes, reducing the risk of dosing errors.

3. **Ease of Use:**

- *Advantage:* Pens are user-friendly, with simple mechanisms for dose adjustment and injection, making them suitable for people of all ages.

5. **No Need for External Devices:**

- *Advantage:* Unlike insulin pumps, pens do not require external devices, making them a simpler option for many people.

In India, there are several insulin pens available. Some common types include:

1. **Disposable Pens:**

2. **Reusable Pens:**

INSULIN ANALOGS

Insulin analogs are like upgraded versions of the natural insulin your body makes. They're made by altering the chemical structures of the Insulin so that it will act more like the insulin your body would produce on its own, helping to control blood sugar levels better. Think of them as the high-tech, more efficient helpers your body needs to keep things in balance.

Various types of Insulin analogs present in the market which are

commonly used:

1. **Rapid-acting insulin analogs:**

2. **Short-acting insulin analog:**

3. **Intermediate-acting insulin analog:**

4. **Long-acting insulin analogs:**

These insulin analogs vary in how quickly they start working, how long they last, and when they peak in terms of effectiveness. It's like having different tools for different jobs!

*Advantages of Insulin Analogs:*

1. **Faster Onset and Shorter Duration (Rapid-acting):**

- Mimics the natural response of the body to meals more closely, helping control post-meal blood sugar spikes.

2. **Stable Basal Coverage (Long-acting):**

Provides a steady release of insulin over an extended period, reducing the need for multiple injections.

3. **Reduced Risk of Hypoglycemia:**

Some analogs have a lower risk of causing low blood sugar compared to traditional insulin.

4. **Flexibility in Timing:**

Can be injected closer to mealtime, offering more flexibility for people with variable meal schedules.

5. **Reduced Variability:**

More predictable in terms of absorption and action compared to regular insulin.

*Disadvantages of Insulin Analogs:*

1. **Cost:**

Insulin analogs are often more expensive than traditional insulin.

2. **Limited Availability:**

Some analogs may not be as widely available as traditional insulin in certain regions.

3. **Potential for Allergic Reactions:**

Although rare, allergic reactions can occur with insulin analogs.

4. **Need for Refrigeration:**

Some analogs require refrigeration, which can be challenging for people who don't have access to a refrigerator.

It's important to note that the advantages and disadvantages can vary from person to person, and the choice of insulin type depends on individual needs, lifestyle, and preferences. Always consult with a healthcare professional to determine the most suitable insulin regimen.

**Note**

In India and most of the developing countries the most commonly used insulin is conventional insulin which comes in vials and patients have to take them with syringes .

Here are some instructions for patients who are taking insulin to control their blood sugar level better avoiding complications like hypoglycemia or severe hyperglycemia .

1. due to various type of insulin present in while like 40 unit and 100 unit strength and different syringes available like 40 and 100 are you it may cause confusion and can cause dangerous hypoglycemia and or hyperglycemia so use only 40 unit series with 40 unit insulin and hundred unit series with hundred unit insulin.

Never interchange 100 unit series with 40 unit insulin and vice versa.

2.100 unit insulin may sound expensive but it is more dense insulin than 40 are you insulin and the cost of insulin per ml is same with that of 40 unit insulin .

example if you are using a hundred unit insulin then it will cost around 500 rupees in Indian rupee that doesn't mean that it is costly it is because your insulin is 2.5 times more than 40 unit insulin and hence lesser amount of insulin in term of ml when you are using it so if 40 unit while will last for 30 days in any patient and if he will use 100 unit insulin in that case it will last forever 80 days so the cost of unit insulin per unit is same.

3.Always use term unit for measurement of insulin and never use ml this is a common confusion done by various patients which leads to dangerous hypoglycemia

4.Always use a new syringe with every prick of insulin.

5.When taking different types of insulin, always take individual injections and don't mix two types of insulin in one series.

6.Always store insulin in the door of a refrigerator and never keep it in the freezer section of your refrigerator.

7.Bring insulin out of the refrigerator half hour prior to delivery so that it's temperature will get equated with normal room temperature and patients body temperature.

8.Ideal site of insulin injections are either thigh or abdomen never interchange thigh and abdomen during injection .because your blood sugar control varies due to the different absorption mechanism in different areas of body.

9.If a patient doesn't have a refrigerator at home then he may use an earthy container to store the insulin which should be filled with water and kept in a pile of sand.

10.During travel or transportation you can use different pouches available like Frio pouches to keep your insulin in that pouch which when kept wet will last for 8 hours and keep your insulin safe from external temperature.

11.Try to learn the art of giving insulin and take it on your own and don't depend on others so that you will take your own insulin in time.

12.Never think that blood sugar will automatically get controlled with insulin after taking insulin, a lot of work to be done from the patient's side.

13.Never think that insulin once started in pregnancy will be continued for life.

14.Some patient starts insulin and keep taking the same dose of insulin which we give at our clinic throughout life please don't do that insulin dose is to be regularly monitor and altered according to your blood sugar level only taking insulin will not solve the problem but the exit insulin dose will solve your problem and which is to be done by the physician who is looking after you.

15. Don't inject at the same site always but keep rotating the site every time ,it will decrease the incidence of lipoatrophy and ulcer in the skin.

Note: In our clinic we use a method in which you have to tell us your blood sugar level after checking it at home with a help of glucometer and report us through WhatsApp and after seeing the reports we just tell you what should be the amount of insulin you should take which will help you to treat your blood sugar at the comfort of your home.

If you are taking insulin and your blood sugar is not controlled then you can consult us online by calling us in various numbers of our clinic from anywhere in the world.

+91-9040881281

+91-9438226633

E mail: drsklath@gmail.com

**INSULIN PUMPS**

Imagine having a tiny, smart friend helping you manage your diabetes all day long—that's kind of like what an insulin pump does!

An insulin pump is a small device that looks like a little computer or a fancy pager. Instead of giving yourself insulin shots with needles, the pump does it for you. It's like having a constant drip of insulin that you control.

Here's how it works: You fill the pump with insulin and wear it on your body, usually on a belt or in your pocket. It's connected to a small tube (like a straw) that goes under your skin. The pump sends tiny bits of insulin into your body throughout the day, just like your pancreas would if it were working perfectly.

The cool part? You can also tell the pump to give you extra insulin when you eat, just by pressing some buttons. It's like having your own diabetes superhero right there, helping you stay balanced.

People love pumps because they're super convenient, and you don't need to poke yourself with needles all the time. Of course, you'll still need to check your blood sugar and work with your doctor to make sure everything's going smoothly. But overall, insulin pumps are like having a high-tech sidekick in the battle against diabetes!

ADVANTAGES OF INSULIN PUMPS

1. **No More Shots, :**

- With an insulin pump, you don't have to give yourself shots all the time. No more poking yourself with needles—it's a win!

2. **Customizable Doses:**

- You can tell the pump how much insulin you need, especially when you eat. It's like having a personalised diabetes plan that fits your life.

3. **Steady Insulin Flow:**

- The pump gives you a steady flow of insulin throughout the day, just like how your body would do it naturally.

4. **Freedom to Move:**

- You can move around more freely without carrying needles and vials. It's like having a diabetes assistant that goes wherever you go.

5. **Better Blood Sugar Control:**

- Many people find that using a pump helps them keep their blood sugar levels in a better range.

DISADVANTAGES OF INSULIN PUMPS

1. **Wearing it 24/7:**

- Since the pump is attached to you, you have to wear it all the time. Some people might find this a bit bothersome.

2. **Learning Curve:**

- It takes a bit of time to learn how to use the pump and get used to it. But don't worry, practice makes perfect!

3. **Technical Glitches:**

- Sometimes, like any tech, pumps can have technical issues. But the good news is, they usually have backup plans for these situations.

4. **Cost:**

- Insulin pumps can be expensive, and not everyone might be able to afford one.

In the end, insulin pumps can be like having a diabetes superhero on your team. They come with some quirks, but many folks find the benefits outweigh the challenges. Always chat with your healthcare team to figure out if an insulin pump is the right fit for you!

In our clinic, we encounter individuals dealing with diabetes mellitus, each with unique thoughts and feelings.

It's crucial to address two common myths of Diabetic patients :

1. **Ignoring Symptoms Misconception:**

- Some believe that if they don't feel symptoms, their blood sugar is normal.

- The challenge lies in adhering to doctor-recommended actions like diet control, exercise, and medication but the most important is regular check-ups of the patient's blood sugar which will tell the exact Blood sugar status of the patient.

2. **Influence of Questionable Advice:**

- Others follow medical advice but encounter misguided tips from friends.

- Questionable suggestions include skipping prescribed meds, relying solely on exercise, and opting for homemade remedies.

- Following such advice can lead to irreversible complications, emphasising the importance of trusting medical guidance.

# CHAPTER SEVEN

# CLINICAL AND LAB EVALUATION OF A DIABETES PATIENT

*"Monitoring diabetes is the most crucial for managing the condition effectively and preventing complications. Clinical and laboratory (LB) evaluations play a pivotal role in assessing the status of diabetes patients. Let's delve into the aim, methods, advantages, and disadvantages of these evaluations."*

**Aim of Monitoring:**

The primary goal of monitoring diabetes is to maintain optimal blood glucose levels, prevent complications, and enhance the patient's overall well-being. Clinical and LAB evaluations help healthcare providers understand how well a patient is managing their diabetes and if any adjustments to their treatment plan are necessary.

**Methods of Monitoring:**

1. **Clinical Evaluation:**

- *Physical Examination:* Assessing vital signs, body weight, and overall physical health can provide insights into the patient's diabetes management.

- *Symptom Assessment:* Monitoring symptoms such as excessive thirst, frequent urination, and fatigue helps gauge the impact of diabetes on daily life.

We recommend that patients visit the clinic on a monthly basis if their blood sugar levels are not well-controlled. However, for those with stable conditions and normal results, a visit every three months is advised.

2. **Laboratory Evaluation:**

Here are some simplified guidelines for blood sugar measurement for patients:

1. **Fasting Blood Sugar (FBS):**

- **Purpose:** Measures your blood sugar after a period of not eating (usually overnight or 8-10 hrs of no calorie intake).

- **Guideline:** Normal levels are typically between 70-100 mg/dL. If it's consistently higher, it might indicate a need for dietary or medication adjustments.

2. **Postprandial Blood Sugar (PPBS) or After Meals:**

- **Purpose:** Check your blood sugar about 2 hours after eating.

- **Guideline:** Target is usually below 150 mg/dL. Higher levels may suggest a need for dietary changes or medication adjustments.

Regularly monitor Fasting Blood Sugar (FBS) and Postprandial Blood Sugar (PPBS) levels, with a recommended frequency of at least once a month(You can do it by glucometer at home). Additionally, for specific patient categories such as those on insulin therapy or dealing with Gestational Diabetes Mellitus (GDM), follow the prescribed frequency of testing outlined earlier, ensuring a thorough and consistent monitoring routine.

3. **HbA1c (Glycated Haemoglobin):**

- **Purpose:** Reflects your average blood sugar over the past 2-3 months.

- **Guideline:** Try to keep it below 7 %. Higher levels may indicate the need for better diabetes management.

Try to do it every 6 months if Blood sugar is normal and every 3 months if Blood sugar is usually beyond normal level.

4. **Fructosamine Test:**

- **Purpose:** Shows your average blood sugar over the past 2-3 weeks.

- **Guideline:** Normal levels vary but generally below 280 µmol/L. It helps evaluate recent changes in your diabetes management, useful in pregnancy and new insulin or medicine initiation.

5. **Continuous Glucose Monitoring (CGM):**

- **Purpose:** Provides real-time information on your blood sugar throughout the day.

- **Guideline:** Aim for a target range set with your healthcare provider. CGM helps you see trends and make timely adjustments to your diabetes management.

Remember, these are general guidelines, and your healthcare provider will personalise them based on your specific health condition, medications, and lifestyle. Regular communication with your healthcare team is essential for effective diabetes management.

Here I will focus on 2 tests which are vital and should be known by every patient.

"**HbA1c (Haemoglobin A1c):**"

**Test Preparation:**

- **Fasting:** Unlike some other blood tests, HbA1c does not require fasting. You can take the test at any time of the day, with or without food.

- **Regular Medications:** You can continue your regular medications as prescribed unless your healthcare provider advises otherwise. HbA1c reflects your average blood sugar over time, so daily variations won't significantly impact the results.

**Price in India:**

- The cost of an HbA1c test in India can vary depending on the laboratory and location. Generally, it ranges from INR 300 to INR 1000 or more. Some healthcare facilities may offer packages or discounts for multiple tests.

**Advantages:**

1. **Long-Term View:** HbA1c provides a long-term average of blood sugar levels over 2-3 months, offering a comprehensive view of diabetes management.

2. **No Fasting Required:** The convenience of not fasting before the test makes it more accessible and less cumbersome for patients.

3. **Stability:** HbA1c is not affected by short-term factors like recent meals, making it a stable and reliable indicator of overall glucose control.

**Disadvantages:**

1. **Limited Short-Term Insight:** HbA1c doesn't provide real-time information and may not capture short-term fluctuations in blood sugar levels.

2. **Influence of Certain Conditions:** Conditions affecting red blood cell turnover, such as anaemia, can impact the accuracy of HbA1c results.

3. **Individual Variation:** Individual variations in the lifespan of red blood cells can affect the accuracy of the average represented by HbA1c.

In conclusion, HbA1c is a valuable tool for assessing long-term glycemic control in diabetes. Its simplicity in test preparation and stable nature make it widely used in clinical practice. While it has certain limitations, it remains a key component in the management of diabetes, providing important insights for both healthcare providers and patients.

CGMS/AGP

Here I will detail about new technology called CGMS used in some cases of Diabetes Mellitus where the blood sugar fluctuates too much

Continuous Glucose Monitoring Systems (CGMS) are devices that track glucose levels throughout the day and night. Here are some details:

**How to use:**

1. **Sensor Placement:** A small sensor is inserted under the skin, usually on the abdomen.

2. **Data Transmission:** The sensor measures glucose levels according to the preset time and it can be worn for 14 days at a stretch. After 14 days we can transmit data to a receiver or Smartphone and analyse the data in the form of easy to analyse the picture and derive important insights from it.

3.Some newer devices give facility to patients so that they can check their glucose levels in real-time and receive alerts for high or low levels.

**Price:**

The cost varies, but it generally includes the sensor, transmitter, and receiver which costs approximately 5000 to 7000 in India.

**Advantages:**

1. **Real-time Monitoring:** Constant awareness of glucose levels.

2. **Alerts:** Immediate notifications for high or low glucose levels.

3. **Data Analysis:** Detailed reports presented in graphical patterns help in understanding patterns and making informed decisions.

4. **Improved Diabetes Management:** Helps in better managing diabetes with more accurate information.

**Disadvantages:**

1. **Cost:** CGMS can be expensive, and not everyone may have insurance coverage.

2. **Sensor Insertion:** Some may find the insertion process uncomfortable.

3. **Calibration:** Calibration may be required, and accuracy can be affected if not done properly.

4. **Skin Irritation:** Some users may experience skin irritation around the sensor site.

**Where to do:**

CGMS devices are typically prescribed by healthcare professionals. You can get them through pharmacies, medical supply stores, or directly from the manufacturers.

**SUMMARY**

Note: Most of the patient fails to do regular blood sugar check up So we prefer them to do it at their home with Good quality Glucometer like Bayer, One touch Or accu check frequently whenever you are getting time and note it down and if you find sugar levels beyond normal range IE: fasting above 120 or ppbs above 150 contact your Doctor immediately.

Here i want to put emphasis on HBA1C as most of the patients are unaware of it, so please go through it in details as in most of the cases you need only 2 tests

1.FBS & PPBS through lab or via glucometer

2.HbA1c

# CHAPTER EIGHT

# COMPLICATIONS OF DIABETES

*"2 TYPES:*
*1.Chronic*
*2.Acute*
*(Chronic:Takes time to develop)"*

Chronuic Types:
**Macro vascular Complications**
- Atherosclerosis
- Coronary Artery Disease (CAD)
- Peripheral Arterial Disease (PAD)
- Stroke
**Micro vascular Complications**
- Diabetic Retinopathy
- Diabetic Nephropathy
- Diabetic Neuropathy
**Neurological Complications**
- Autonomic Neuropathy
- Peripheral Neuropathy
**Cardiovascular Complications**
- Hypertension

- Cardiomyopathy
**Metabolic Complications**
- Ketoacidosis
- Hyperosmolar Hyperglycemic State (HHS)
**Skin Complications**
- Diabetic Dermopathy
- Necrobiosis Lipoidica Diabeticorum
**Gastrointestinal Complications**
- Gastroparesis
**Infections**
- Skin Infections
- Urinary Tract Infections (UTIs)
- Fungal Infections
**Mental Health Complications**
- Depression
- Anxiety

These are just a few examples, and it's important for individuals with diabetes to work closely with healthcare professionals to manage and prevent these complications.

Let us discuss the important complications in detail

## "*CAD (CORONARY ARTERY DISEASES*"

Coronary Artery Disease (CAD) occurs when the blood vessels that provide oxygen to the heart muscle narrow or block due to the accumulation of fatty deposits known as plaque. Factors contributing to plaque formation include elevated sugar levels, high blood pressure, a sedentary lifestyle, elevated cholesterol, obesity, and smoking.

This restriction in blood flow can lead to chest pain (angina) or, in severe cases, a heart attack. Lifestyle changes, medications, and interventions like angioplasty or bypass surgery are common approaches to manage CAD and reduce the risk of complications. Regular medical check-ups and adopting a heart-healthy lifestyle are crucial for managing and preventing coronary artery disease.

**Symptoms:**

- Stable angina (In early stages where chest pain which occurs only with regular exercise and movement only )

This is the most important stage as early diagnosis and treatment at this stage can prevent a deadly heart attack.

- Shortness of breath.

- Fatigue.

- Asymptomatic(Many patient do not have any symptom of Angina Or Heart attack)

- Chest pain or discomfort (angina) at rest is called Unstable Angina or Heart attack when the initial stage is not being taken care of.

**Diagnosis:**

- Electrocardiogram (ECG/EKG).

- Stress test (Treadmill test)

- Coronary angiography.

- Blood tests for cardiac markers.

**Treatment:**

- Medications to control diabetes, blood pressure, and cholesterol and reduce the chest pain with medicines

- Lifestyle modifications (healthy diet, exercise).

- Angioplasty or stent placement for severe cases.

- Coronary artery bypass surgery if necessary.

Remember in early stages you may not have any symptoms and resting ECG may come normal particularly if you don't do regular exercise, In such cases do a Treadmill test every 1 yr to diagnose this condition at an early stage.

Remember, early detection and proactive management are key in reducing the impact of diabetes-related CAD and

Atherosclerosis. Regular check-ups and a healthy lifestyle can make a significant difference

MYTHS ASSOCIATED WITH CAD

- **Over Reliance on Medication:** Some patients may mistakenly believe that medication alone is sufficient to prevent a heart attack, neglecting the importance of lifestyle changes.

- **Ignoring Symptoms:** Some individuals with coronary artery disease (CAD) may downplay or ignore symptoms such as chest pain or shortness of breath, attributing them to other causes.

- **Poor Diet Choices:** Many patients may not fully understand the impact of diet on heart health. Consuming a diet high in saturated and trans fats, sodium, and low in fruits and vegetables can contribute to the progression of CAD.

- **Inadequate Exercise:** Some patients may underestimate the significance of regular physical activity in managing CAD. Sedentary lifestyles can contribute to weight gain and worsen cardiovascular health.

- **Smoking and Tobacco Use:** Continuing to smoke or use tobacco products can significantly increase the risk of a heart attack. Some patients may struggle to quit despite the known health risks.

- **Stress Mismanagement:** Failing to effectively manage stress can exacerbate CAD. Patients may not prioritise stress-reducing activities such as relaxation techniques or hobbies.

- **Inconsistent Medication Adherence:** Some patients may forget or choose not to take prescribed medications regularly, putting themselves at a higher risk of a cardiac event.

- **Lack of Regular Check-ups:** Avoiding regular medical check-ups can result in missed opportunities to monitor and manage CAD. Routine evaluations help catch potential issues early on.

- **Disregarding Weight Management:** Maintaining a healthy weight is crucial for heart health. Some patients may struggle with weight management, which can contribute to the progression of CAD.

- **Delaying Medical Attention:** In the event of new or worsening symptoms, some patients may delay seeking medical attention, hoping the issue will resolve on its own. This delay can be dangerous in the case of a heart attack.

Remember, it's essential for CAD patients to adopt a holistic approach, combining medication with lifestyle changes and regular medical monitoring.

Important practical points :

1. Many patients believe that if their ECG results are normal, their heart is fine. However, it's not entirely true. ECG can only detect heart problems when the heart is at rest. In early coronary artery disease (CAD), the resting blood flow appears normal. In such cases, a treadmill test or angiography becomes essential to identify blockages in the coronary arteries.

2. Some patients think they don't need to worry about heart disease because they don't experience symptoms. It's important to note that diabetic patients with autonomic neuropathy may not feel chest pain. Even without chest pain, it's crucial to undergo a cardiac check-up annually to prevent the progression of coronary artery disease and potential heart attacks.

3. Patients often stop exercising when they encounter chest pain or shortness of breath. This is counterproductive as it can lead to the development of more atherosclerosis

in the coronary arteries, making blockages more prominent and increasing the risk of a heart attack. Instead of stopping exercise, consult your doctor to uncover any hidden heart blockages.

4. Many patients dismiss chest pain at night, attributing it to gas or acidity. Delaying a doctor consultation by hours, days, or weeks can be detrimental, especially when chest pain is accompanied by shortness of breath, sweating, and a cold body. Seek immediate medical attention, even at night, to prevent further damage or death. In remote areas, don't wait for an ambulance; use your vehicle to reach the nearest medical facility promptly.

5. Patients with a history of bypass surgery or coronary artery stenting may mistakenly believe they are immune to future heart disease or heart attacks. Some continue their pre-heart attack lifestyle, while others adopt new unhealthy habits. It's crucial to recognize that a history of heart procedures doesn't guarantee immunity. Lifestyle changes are necessary to prevent the recurrence of heart attacks and, in some cases, death.

6. As per certain guidelines, cholesterol-lowering medications are often prescribed to individuals, even if their cholesterol levels are within the normal range. Some patients may discontinue these medications, considering them unnecessary, but it's important to follow medical advice.

7. Ignoring the significance of cholesterol-lowering medications can pose a risk of heart attack. Patients should refrain from discontinuing these medications without consulting their healthcare provider to ensure continued heart protection.

8. The heart is a vital organ, and many patients succumb to heart attacks due to negligence. It is crucial to

consistently care for your heart and take preventive measures to avoid the risks associated with heart attacks.

## "*DIABETIC CARDIOMYOPATHY*"

Diabetic Cardiomyopathy is a condition where diabetes affects the heart muscle, leading to structural and functional changes and weakness of Heart. Over time, it can result in heart failure and other cardiovascular complications.

*Symptoms:*
- Fatigue
- Shortness of breath
- Swelling in the legs and ankles
-Dyspnea on exertion
-Dyspnea during sleep
-Cough during sleep

*Prevention and Management:*
- **Blood Sugar Control:**
- **Regular Monitoring:** Keep a close eye on blood pressure and cholesterol levels.
- **Lifestyle Modifications:** Adopt a heart-healthy lifestyle with a balanced diet, regular exercise, and weight management.
- **Medication Adherence:** Take prescribed medications consistently and as directed by healthcare providers.

*Regular Check-ups:*
- Schedule regular check-ups with your healthcare team to monitor heart health and diabetes management.

*Seek Medical Attention:*
If you experience symptoms like chest pain, severe fatigue, or difficulty breathing, seek immediate medical

attention.

Remember, early detection and proactive management play a crucial role in maintaining heart health, especially for individuals with diabetes.

## "*STROKE*"

In layman's terms we also call it paralysis where one part of your body or one half of your body stops working.

**Importance:**

- Stroke is a severe complication of diabetes, requiring immediate attention.

- It occurs when blood flow to the brain is disrupted, leading to potential long-term damage or death.

**Symptoms and Signs:**

- Sudden numbness or weakness on one side of the body or any part of the body.

- Confusion or difficulty speaking

- Trouble walking

- Severe headache

- Difficulty in swallowing

- Abnormal vision

**Diagnosis:**

- Swift diagnosis through imaging tests like CT scans or MRIs.

- Blood tests to identify underlying causes, such as high blood sugar.

**Risk Factors:**

- Diabetes increases stroke risk.

- High blood pressure, high cholesterol, smoking, obesity, and sedentary lifestyle contribute.

**Prevention:**

- Control blood sugar, blood pressure, and cholesterol.

- Adopt a heart-healthy lifestyle with regular exercise and a balanced diet.
- Avoid smoking to significantly reduce stroke risk.
**Treatment:**
- Immediate medical attention is crucial within hours.
- Medications or procedures to dissolve clots or repair blood vessels.
- Rehabilitation, including physical and occupational therapy, for recovery.

MYTHS AND MISTAKES IN PREVENTION OF STROKE:

- **Belief in a Specific Age Limit:** Some individuals mistakenly think that strokes only affect the elderly. In reality, strokes can occur at any age, and awareness and prevention efforts should be a lifelong priority.

- **Neglecting Hypertension Management:** High blood pressure is a significant risk factor for strokes, yet some patients may not consistently monitor or manage their blood pressure, leading to an increased risk.

- **Ignoring the Role of Diet:** A common mistake is underestimating the impact of diet on stroke prevention. Poor dietary choices, especially those high in salt and saturated fats, can contribute to hypertension and other risk factors.

- **Lack of Regular Exercise:** Sedentary lifestyles contribute to various risk factors for stroke, such as obesity and hypertension. Some individuals may not realise the importance of regular physical activity in stroke prevention.

- **Disregarding Symptoms:** Ignoring warning signs such as sudden severe headaches, numbness, or difficulty speaking can be a critical mistake. Quick medical attention is crucial for minimising the damage caused by a stroke.

- **Not Managing Diabetes Effectively:** Individuals with diabetes have an increased risk of stroke. Inadequate management of blood sugar levels can contribute to this risk.

- **Smoking and Tobacco Use:** Some patients may underestimate the impact of smoking on stroke risk. Smoking damages blood vessels and contributes to the buildup of plaque, increasing the likelihood of a stroke.

- **Excessive Alcohol Consumption:** Consuming alcohol in excess can raise blood pressure and contribute to other risk factors for stroke. Some individuals may overlook the connection between alcohol and stroke.

- **Inconsistent Medication Adherence:** Patients prescribed medications for conditions like atrial fibrillation or anticoagulants may not consistently take their medications, leaving them vulnerable to stroke.

- **Neglecting Regular Health Check-ups:** Skipping routine medical check-ups means missing opportunities to monitor and manage risk factors. Regular health assessments help catch and address potential issues early on.

Educating individuals about these myths and mistakes is crucial for promoting stroke awareness and prevention. It's essential for patients to adopt a comprehensive approach that includes a healthy lifestyle, regular medical check-ups, and adherence to prescribed medications.

Detecting subtle symptoms before full-blown paralysis is crucial. Look out for signs like confusion, difficulty in speaking or working, a tendency to fall, and weakness in one side of the hand, face, or leg. Once you notice these subtle symptoms, consult your doctor promptly. Taking proactive steps can prevent further brain damage and the eventual development of paralysis.

In the event of a stroke or paralysis, there's a critical three-hour window from the onset of weakness. During this time, administering blood-thinning drugs can completely reverse paralysis. However, a thorough physical examination and a CT scan are necessary, consuming valuable time. If you experience weakness, don't delay—seek immediate medical attention. Even if paralysis occurs at midnight, waiting until morning is not an option. The crucial three-hour timeframe requires a swift journey to the hospital.

It's important to understand that waiting until after paralysis occurs to seek treatment is not effective. Once paralysis develops, its improvement is crucial, and no specific medicines can treat it. The improvement is a natural process, and no external treatment can alter its course. Avoid searching for a specific treatment, once you develop full blown paralysis .

Following a stroke, some patients tend to seek treatment solely for the current episode of paralysis, overlooking the crucial aspect of addressing risk factors. It's essential to shift the focus towards understanding and managing these risk factors, as they play a significant role in the potential development of further episodes of paralysis or stroke. Rather than solely emphasising the treatment of the present stroke episode, consider taking proactive measures to mitigate the risk factors associated with future incidents. This holistic approach ensures a more comprehensive and long-term strategy for stroke prevention and overall well-being.

*"DIABETIC EYE DISEASE"*

**Importance:**
- Diabetes increases the risk of vision complications.
- Diabetic Eye Disease is a leading cause of permanent blindness in adults.

**Symptoms:**
- Blurred or fluctuating vision.
- Floaters (spots or dark strings in vision).
- Difficulty seeing at night.
- Eye pain or pressure.
- Asymptomatic in early stages

**Diagnosis:**
- Comprehensive eye exam.
- Dilated eye exam.
- Fluorescein angiography.
- Optical coherence tomography (OCT).

**Prevention:**
- Strict blood sugar control.
- Regular eye exams (at least once a year).
- Blood pressure and cholesterol management.
- Quit smoking.
- Protect eyes from excessive sunlight.

**Treatment:**
- Laser therapy for retinopathy.
- Intravitreal injections for macular edema.
- Cataract surgery if needed.
- Glaucoma medications or surgery.

**Early detection and proactive management are crucial to preserving vision in individuals with diabetes. Regular eye check-ups and a healthy lifestyle can significantly reduce the risk of diabetic eye complications.**

MYTHS AND MISTAKES:

- **Assuming Good Vision Means Healthy Eyes:** Some individuals believe that as long as their vision is clear, their eyes must be healthy. However, retinopathy can develop without noticeable symptoms in the early stages.

- **Neglecting Regular Eye Exams:** Patients may skip regular eye exams, assuming that vision screenings are sufficient. Comprehensive eye exams are crucial for detecting conditions like retinopathy early on.

- **Delaying Treatment:** If retinopathy is diagnosed, some patients may delay or avoid recommended treatments such as laser therapy or injections, assuming the condition will resolve on its own

- **Believing Only Severe Diabetes Leads to Retinopathy:** Some individuals think that only those with severe or long-standing diabetes are at risk of retinopathy. However, the condition can occur in individuals with less severe forms of diabetes as well.

- **Not Protecting Eyes from UV Rays:** Neglecting to wear sunglasses that block harmful UV rays can contribute to eye damage, including retinopathy. UV protection is essential for overall eye health.

- **Assuming Eye Symptoms are Normal Ageing:** Patients may dismiss symptoms like floaters, flashes of light, or changes in vision as normal signs of ageing, ignoring potential signs of retinopathy.

Education and awareness about retinopathy and its prevention are crucial for patients, especially those with diabetes. Encouraging regular eye check-ups, optimal blood sugar control, and a healthy lifestyle can contribute to the prevention and early detection of retinopathy.

In essence, it's essential to undergo an annual eye checkup with an ophthalmologist to promptly detect any signs of retinopathy which is the most important complication of Diabetes. It's crucial not to mistake this for a routine eye examination for glasses, a common error made by many patients.

## "*KIDNEY DISEASE*"

**Introduction:**
Diabetic Kidney Disease (DKD) is a serious complication that can arise from long-term diabetes. This condition occurs when diabetes damages the kidneys, affecting their ability to filter waste products and excess fluids from the blood. Understanding the importance of early detection, symptoms, diagnosis, and effective management is crucial for individuals living with diabetes.

**Importance:**
Diabetic Kidney Disease is a leading cause of kidney failure worldwide. Managing diabetes effectively is key to preventing or slowing down the progression of DKD. Early intervention can significantly improve outcomes and enhance the quality of life for individuals with diabetes.

**Symptoms:**
DKD often develops gradually and may not show noticeable symptoms in its early stages. However, as the condition progresses, individuals may experience swelling in the ankles, fatigue, changes in urination frequency, and elevated blood pressure.

**How to Diagnose:**
Regular monitoring and screening for kidney function are essential for individuals with diabetes. The following diagnostic tests are commonly used:

1. **Blood Tests:** Measures creatinine levels to assess kidney function.

2. **Urinalysis:** Checks for the presence of protein in the urine, an early sign of kidney damage.

3. **Glomerular Filtration Rate (GFR):** Determines how well the kidneys are filtering waste from the blood.

**Normal Lab Values:**

- **Creatinine levels:** 0.6 to 1.3 mg/dL for men, 0.5 to 1.1 mg/dL for women.

- **GFR:** A normal GFR is 90 or above.

**Other Risk Factors:**

Several factors can increase the risk of developing DKD, including genetics, high blood pressure, smoking, and poor diabetes management. Controlling these risk factors is crucial for preventing complications.

**Treatment:**

1. **Blood Sugar Control:** Maintaining target blood glucose levels is vital in slowing down the progression of DKD.

2. **Blood Pressure Management:** Keeping blood pressure within a healthy range (usually below 130/80 mmHg) is crucial to protect the kidneys.

3. **Medications:** Angiotensin-converting enzyme (ACE) inhibitors and angiotensin II receptor blockers (ARBs) may be prescribed to manage blood pressure and protect the kidneys.

**Dos and Don'ts:**

- **Do:** Follow a balanced diet, exercise regularly, take medications as prescribed, and attend regular check-ups.

- **Don't:** Neglect your diabetes management, skip medications, ignore symptoms, or consume excessive amounts of salt.

**Conclusion:**

Diabetic Kidney Disease is a serious complication, but with proactive management and lifestyle changes, its progression can be slowed down or even prevented. Regular monitoring, early intervention, and a collaborative effort between healthcare professionals and individuals with diabetes are essential in the fight against DKD. If you have diabetes, prioritise your kidney health by staying informed, adopting a healthy lifestyle, and seeking timely medical advice.

Certainly! Glomerular Filtration Rate (GFR) is a key indicator of kidney function, representing the rate at which the kidneys filter blood. GFR is measured in millilitres per minute per 1.73 square metres of body surface area (ml/min/1.73m²). The normal GFR range is typically considered to be 90 or above.

Here's an elaboration on GFR values:
1. **Normal GFR (90 or above):**
2. **Mildly Decreased GFR (60-89):**
3. **Moderately Decreased GFR (30-59):**
4. **Severely Decreased GFR (15-29):**
5. **Kidney Failure (GFR less than 15):**
- A GFR below 15 indicates kidney failure. Individuals with kidney failure often require dialysis or kidney transplantation to sustain life. Palliative care may also be considered to enhance the quality of life.

It's important to note that GFR values are just one aspect of assessing kidney function. Other factors, such as creatinine levels and urinalysis, are also considered in conjunction with GFR to provide a comprehensive understanding of kidney health. Regular monitoring of GFR is crucial for individuals with diabetes, hypertension, or other conditions that can impact kidney function, as it allows for early detection and intervention to prevent or slow down the progression of kidney disease.

**MYTHS AND MISTAKES:**

- **Belief in Symptom-Free Safety:** Some individuals mistakenly assume that as long as they don't experience symptoms, their kidneys must be healthy. However, kidney disease can progress silently without obvious signs in the early stages.

- **Inadequate Hydration:** Some patients underestimate the importance of staying adequately hydrated. Dehydration can contribute to kidney damage, and maintaining proper fluid balance is crucial for kidney health.

- **Ignoring High Blood Pressure:** Hypertension is a leading cause of kidney disease, yet some individuals may not prioritise blood pressure management, overlooking its impact on kidney function.

- **Poorly Managed Diabetes:** Patients with diabetes may not fully understand the connection between diabetes and kidney disease. Inadequate blood sugar control can contribute to the development and progression of diabetic nephropathy.

- **Overuse of Painkillers:** Excessive use of over-the-counter painkillers, especially non-steroidal anti-inflammatory drugs (NSAIDs), can contribute to kidney damage. Some patients may not be aware of the potential risks associated with these medications.

- **Excessive Salt Consumption:** High salt intake can contribute to hypertension and kidney damage. Some individuals may not realise the importance of a low-sodium diet in kidney disease prevention.

- **Ignoring Family History:** Patients with a family history of kidney disease may overlook the genetic component and assume they are not at risk. Awareness of family history is crucial for early detection and prevention.

- **Skipping Regular Check-ups:** Neglecting routine medical check-ups means missed opportunities to monitor kidney function. Regular screenings help detect issues early on when interventions can be more effective.

- **Lack of Exercise:** Sedentary lifestyles contribute to various risk factors for kidney disease, such as obesity and hypertension. Regular physical activity is essential for overall kidney health.

- **Delaying Medical Attention:** Some individuals may delay seeking medical help when experiencing urinary or kidney-related symptoms, assuming the issues will resolve on their own. Early intervention is key in managing kidney disease.

Educating patients about these myths and mistakes is essential for kidney disease prevention. Emphasising the importance of a healthy lifestyle, regular check-ups, and managing underlying health conditions can contribute to maintaining optimal kidney function.

Practical points:

1. In the early stages, kidney disease may not show symptoms. Many patients solely rely on serum urea and creatinine tests to assess their kidney health. However, they often neglect other critical factors such as blood sugar and blood pressure, leading to eventual renal failure. This, in turn, necessitates treatments like dialysis or renal transplantation. Rather than focusing solely on creatinine levels, it's crucial to pay attention to the aforementioned risk factors.

2.Along with the conventional creatinine test, consider the microalbumin or urine albumin-creatinine ratio. This test reveals the amount of protein reaching your kidneys. I'm presenting a brief piece on the albumin-creatinine ratio test, a vital diagnostic tool that every patient should undergo to identify kidney disease.

3. Kidney damage is a preventable condition; unfortunately, it cannot be reversed once it occurs. The key is to take proactive measures to safeguard your kidneys from harm.

4. Some individuals believe that if they experience kidney discomfort, they can seek treatment for kidney disease. It's important to note that kidney damage is irreversible. If your kidneys are damaged, the deterioration will persist over a few years, leading to various complications.

5. Kidneys perform numerous functions beyond urine production. If they fail, you may experience anaemia, uncontrolled blood pressure, electrolyte imbalance, cardiac abnormalities, sudden cardiac death, acid-base abnormalities, disruptions in brain function, and imbalances in calcium and vitamin D levels in your body.

ACR(Albumin creatinine ratio) :

**Monitoring Kidney Health: The ACR Test for Diabetes Patients**

**Importance:**

- The Albumin Creatinine Ratio (ACR) test is a vital tool for assessing kidney health in diabetes patients.

- Early detection of kidney issues allows for timely intervention and prevention of complications.

**What is ACR?**

- A urine test measuring the ratio of albumin (a protein) to creatinine (a waste product) in urine.

**Why is it Important for Diabetes Patients?**

- Diabetes is a major contributor to kidney disease, making regular ACR tests crucial for early detection of diabetic nephropathy (kidney damage).

**When to Take the Test:**

- Recommended annually for diabetes patients to monitor kidney health.

**How is the Test Done?**

- A simple urine sample collected during a routine check-up.

**Interpreting Results:**

- Normal ACR levels: Less than 30 mg/g (milligrams per gram) of creatinine.

- Elevated levels may indicate kidney damage, necessitating further evaluation.

**Cost**

-Approx 500 rupees in INR

**Conclusion:**

Regular ACR testing empowers diabetes patients to proactively manage their kidney health. Understanding and maintaining normal ACR levels are key steps in preventing complications associated with diabetic kidney disease.

## "NEUROPATHY (nerve damage)"

**Importance:**

- Diabetes increases the risk of nerve damage.

- Diabetic Neuropathy affects the nerves throughout the body.

**Symptoms:**

- Numbness or tingling in the extremities and sometimes burning or sharp pain which ultimately leads to complete nerve damage of foot and legs leading to inability to know the presence of earth below your feet and tendency to fall .

-Developing foot ulcers due to inability to sense small pins, stones in your shoes, which ultimately leads to chronic non healing ulcer and amputation of feet in some cases.

- Muscle weakness of legs

- weakness of eye muscles leading to difficulty in moving the eyeball

-Autonomic nerve damage of heart which is most dangerous and commonly neglected neuropathy leading to

- Abnormal increase or decrease of heart rate

- Lack of chest pain in heart attack,

- Syncope and repeated fall,

-Autonomic neuropathy of GI tract leading to

- Chronic constipation

- chronic diarrhoea

- faecal incontinence leading to repeated soiling of clothes.

-Nerve damage of Genitourinary organs which is most disabling and most of the people don't speak about it may lead to

- Impotence

- Neurogenic bladder leading to urinary incontinence

- Retrograde and dry ejaculation.

-Truncal neuropathy leading to pain abdomen which is not cured by standard pain abdomen medicines

**Diagnosis:**

Various tests may be advised like

- Clinical evaluation by a healthcare provider.

- Nerve conduction studies.

- Electromyography (EMG).

- Imaging tests (CT scan or MRI) in some cases.

**Risk Factors:**

- Poorly controlled blood sugar.
- Diabetes duration.
- Smoking.
- High blood pressure.
- Obesity.

**Prevention:**

- Maintain optimal blood sugar levels.
- Regular foot care and inspections.
- Manage blood pressure and cholesterol.
- Avoid smoking.
- Regular exercise to promote circulation.
-Frequent examination of nerve supply of legs and feet

**Treatment:**

- Medications for pain management only because nerve damage is irreversible so you can only decrease the symptoms and for that you may have to take lifelong medicines.

- Physical therapy to improve muscle strength and coordination.

- Lifestyle modifications (healthy diet, exercise).

- Regular monitoring of feet for early detection of issues.

- Supportive footwear to prevent injuries.

Prevention ,Early detection and proactive management are essential in preventing and managing Diabetic Neuropathy. Regular check-ups and a focus on overall health can significantly improve nerve-related complications in individuals with diabetes.

Role of Vitamin B12 in treatment of Diabetic Neuropathy:

In most cases of diabetic neuropathy, vitamin B12 may not be the primary solution for treatment. While B12 is crucial for nerve health, diabetic neuropathy is a complex condition influenced by various factors, including prolonged high blood sugar levels, inflammation, and vascular issues. If the neuropathy is primarily caused by uncontrolled diabetes or other underlying factors, addressing those root causes becomes paramount.

In such instances, a comprehensive approach focusing on blood sugar management, lifestyle changes, and potentially other targeted medications may take precedence over vitamin B12 supplementation.

## *"SEXUAL DYSFUNCTION"*

**Erectile dysfunction, or the inability to achieve an erection during sexual intercourse, is a common complication in diabetic males. Unfortunately, many patients may not talk about it with their doctor due to shyness and fear. It's important for patients to openly discuss this complication with their physicians without any hesitation.**

Erectile dysfunction occurs when the nerves and blood vessels in the penis are damaged. In diabetes, these tissues can get damaged, leading to difficulties in getting or maintaining an erection for sexual activity.

There may be other factors contributing to this issue, such as the use of certain drugs, alcohol, hormonal disorders, or psychological problems. These factors can be identified through discussions with your doctor.

To determine the cause of sexual dysfunction, the doctor will conduct a physical examination and perform blood tests and other assessments.

Management:

Certainly! Here's a concise overview of the management of sexual dysfunction in diabetes patients in bullet points:

- **Blood Sugar Control:**

- Maintain optimal blood glucose levels to prevent damage to blood vessels and nerves.

- **Lifestyle Modifications:**

- Adopt a healthy lifestyle with regular exercise, a balanced diet, and weight management to improve overall vascular health.

- **Medication Review:**

- Evaluate and adjust diabetes medications as some may contribute to sexual dysfunction.

- **Address Psychological Factors:**

- Consider counselling or therapy to address any psychological factors contributing to sexual issues.

- **Phosphodiesterase Inhibitors (PDE5 Inhibitors):**

- Medications like sildenafil (Viagra), tadalafil (Cialis), or vardenafil (Levitra) may be prescribed to enhance blood flow and treat erectile dysfunction.

- **Hormone Therapy:**

- Testosterone replacement therapy may be considered if low testosterone levels are identified.

- **Nitric Oxide Donors:**

- Nitroglycerin or other nitric oxide donors may be used under medical supervision to improve blood flow.

- **Vacuum Devices or Penile Implants:**

- These mechanical devices can be options for men with erectile dysfunction who do not respond to other treatments.

- **Regular Check-ups:**

- Regularly monitor and review the patient's overall health, diabetes management, and any changes in sexual function.

*"DIABETIC FOOT"*

It is the most common complication of Diabetes mellitus leading to significant morbidity and mortality.

So let us discuss the salient points here.

**Aetiology:**

- Diabetic foot ulcers result from nerve damage (neuropathy) and poor blood circulation (vascular issues) associated with diabetes.

**Risk Factors:**

- Prolonged duration of diabetes
- Poorly controlled blood sugar levels
- Peripheral neuropathy (nerve damage)
- Peripheral vascular disease (poor blood circulation)
- Foot deformities
- History of previous foot ulcers
-smoking
-visual impairment

**Precipitating Factors:**

- Trauma or injury to the foot
- Ill-fitting shoes
- Infections
- Calluses or corns
- Barefoot walking
- Improper nail cutting
- Self made surgery of Corn and calluses

**Management:**

- Wound care and dressings
- Antibiotics if infection is present
- Offloading pressure from the affected area
- Blood sugar control
- Vascular interventions if needed

**Prevention:**

- Regular foot examinations
- Proper foot hygiene

- Choosing appropriate footwear with broad front shoes
- Use silicon insoles to prevent foot damage
- Blood sugar control
- Regular exercise to improve circulation
**Do's:**
- Inspect feet daily at night for cuts, sores, or changes and consult immediately if any problems are found.
- Keep feet clean and dry
- Wear well-fitting, comfortable shoes
- Trim toenails carefully
- Seek medical attention for any foot issues promptly
**Don'ts:**
- Avoid walking barefoot, especially in high-risk areas
- Do not attempt to self-treat foot ulcers without professional guidance
- Avoid tight or constricting footwear
**General Advice for Foot Care:**
- Choose shoes with a wide toe box and good arch support
- Moisturize feet, but avoid applying between the toes
- Regularly visit a podiatrist or healthcare provider for foot checks

## "*SKIN DISEASES*"

**Aetiology:**
- Diabetic skin diseases are often linked to complications arising from diabetes, including poor blood circulation, nerve damage, and compromised immune function.
**Risk Factors:**
- Prolonged duration of diabetes
- Poorly controlled blood sugar levels

- Obesity
- Peripheral neuropathy
- Reduced immune function
**Precipitating Factors:**
- Dry skin
- Fungal infections
- Bacterial infections
- Poor wound healing
**Management:**
- Topical medications for skin conditions
- Antibiotics for bacterial infections
- Antifungal medications for fungal infections
- Blood sugar control
- Consultation with a dermatologist for specialised care
**Prevention:**
- Maintain good blood sugar control
- Keep skin clean and moisturised
- Regular skin checks for any abnormalities
- Prompt treatment of wounds or infections
**Do's:**
- Keep skin well-moisturised
- Wear loose, breathable clothing
- Practise good hygiene
- Attend regular dermatology check-ups
- Report any skin changes promptly to healthcare providers
**Don'ts:**
- Avoid scratching itchy skin vigorously
- Do not ignore cuts, bruises, or wounds; treat them promptly
- Avoid tight or restrictive clothing
**General Advice for Skin Care:**
- Choose mild soaps and cleansers

- Pat skin dry instead of rubbing
- Wear sunscreen to protect against sun damage
- Avoid hot baths that may dry out the skin

## "DIABETIC JOINT DISEASES"

**Aetiology:**
- Diabetic joint disease, or diabetic arthropathy, is primarily caused by the long-term effects of diabetes on joints, leading to degeneration, inflammation, and reduced joint function.
**Incidence in India:**
- Diabetic joint diseases are increasingly prevalent in India, reflecting the growing number of diabetes cases in the population.
**Risk Factors:**
- Prolonged duration of diabetes
- Poorly controlled blood sugar levels
- Obesity
- Peripheral neuropathy
- Reduced blood circulation
**Precipitating Factors:**
- Chronic inflammation in the joints
- Impaired joint lubrication
- Weakened cartilage and connective tissues
- Nerve damage affecting joint sensation
**Types of Diabetic Joint Diseases:**
1. **Charcot Arthropathy:** Involves joint deformities and fractures due to nerve damage.
2. **Frozen Shoulder (Adhesive Capsulitis):** Causes stiffness and limited motion in the shoulder joint.
3. **Dupuytren's Contracture:** Leads to the thickening and tightening of tissues in the hand.

3. **Trigger finger:** locking of finger in flexion.
**Management:**
- Pain management with medications
- Physical therapy to improve joint mobility
- Blood sugar control
- Joint injections for inflammation
- Surgical interventions in severe cases
**Do's:**
- Participate in low-impact exercises such as swimming or walking
- Follow a joint-friendly diet rich in nutrients
- Attend regular check-ups with healthcare providers
- Use assistive devices if necessary for joint support
**Don'ts:**
- Avoid excessive strain on joints
- Do not ignore joint pain or stiffness
- Limit activities that may worsen joint discomfort
**General Advice for Joint Care:**
- Choose comfortable and supportive footwear
- Practise joint-friendly movements
- Use proper body mechanics to avoid joint stress
- Stay well-hydrated for joint lubrication

Remember, early intervention and a holistic approach to joint health are crucial in managing diabetic joint diseases. Regular communication with healthcare providers ensures tailored care for individual needs.

SPECIAL MENTION ON FROZEN SHOULDER :
**Aetiology:**
- Diabetic frozen shoulder, also known as adhesive capsulitis, is characterised by the thickening and tightening of the shoulder joint capsule, leading to stiffness and restricted motion.
**Management:**

- Pain management with medications
- Physical therapy to improve range of motion
- Joint injections for inflammation
- Heat or ice therapy
- In severe cases, surgical intervention may be considered

**Exercises for Diabetic Frozen Shoulder:**

1. **Pendulum Stretch:**
- Stand and lean over, supporting the unaffected arm on a table.
- Allow the affected arm to hang freely and make circular motions.

2. **Towel Stretch:**
- Hold a towel behind your back with one hand.
- Use the opposite hand to grab the lower end of the towel.
- Gently pull upward to stretch the affected arm.

3. **External Rotation Stretch:**
- Hold a wand or rod with both hands.
- Lift the wand upward with the unaffected arm, gently stretching the affected arm behind the back.

**Do's:**
- Perform recommended shoulder exercises regularly
- Use heat packs to alleviate stiffness
- Follow the prescribed medication regimen

**Don'ts:**
- Avoid sudden or excessive shoulder movements
- Do not ignore persistent shoulder pain or stiffness
- Limit activities that worsen shoulder discomfort

Remember, consistent exercise, proper management, and early intervention play a crucial role in preventing and managing diabetic frozen shoulders. Always consult with healthcare providers for personalised advice and care.

TRIGGER FINGER

**Aetiology:**

- Trigger finger, or stenosing tenosynovitis, is a condition where one of the fingers gets stuck in a bent position, causing pain and difficulty in movement. It occurs when the flexor tendon sheath becomes inflamed and thickened.

**Risk Factors:**

- Diabetes
- Rheumatoid arthritis
- Overuse of the hand and fingers
- Gender (more common in women)
- Age (more common in individuals over 40)

**Precipitating Factors:**

- Repetitive gripping or grasping motions
- Prolonged or forceful use of the fingers
- Presence of conditions like diabetes or arthritis

**Management:**

- Rest and avoiding repetitive finger movements
- Non-steroidal anti-inflammatory drugs (NSAIDs) for pain and inflammation
- Splinting to immobilise the affected finger
- Corticosteroid injections into the tendon sheath
- In severe cases, surgical release of the affected tendon sheath

1. **Finger Tendon Gliding:**

- Gently bend and straighten the fingers, keeping the palm flat.
- Repeat in a slow and controlled manner.

2. **Rubber Band Stretch:**

- Place a rubber band around the fingers.
- Open and close the fingers against the resistance of the rubber band.

3. **Thumb Flexor Stretch:**
- Gently pull the affected finger backward with the opposite hand to stretch the flexor tendon.
**Prevention:**
- Avoid repetitive gripping or forceful hand movements
- Take breaks during activities that strain the fingers
- Maintain hand and finger flexibility through regular exercises
**Do's:**
- Perform recommended finger exercises regularly
- Use a splint as advised by healthcare providers
- Follow the prescribed medication regimen
**Don'ts:**
- Avoid forceful or excessive use of the affected finger
- Do not ignore persistent finger pain or stiffness
- Limit activities that worsen finger discomfort
Consistent exercises, proper management, and early intervention play a crucial role in preventing and managing trigger finger. Always consult with healthcare providers for personalised advice and care.

## "ORAL PROBLEMS IN DIABETES MELLITUS"

**Importance:**
- Diabetes increases the risk of oral and dental issues.
- Oral health is crucial for overall well-being.
**Symptoms:**
- Persistent bad breath.
- Bleeding gums.
- Dry mouth.
- Tooth sensitivity.
**Signs:**
- Gingivitis (inflammation of the gums).

- Periodontitis (gum disease).
- Tooth decay.
- Delayed wound healing in the oral cavity.
**Diagnosis:**
- Dental examination by a dentist.
- X-rays for detailed assessment.
- Periodontal probing to check for pocket depth.
- Oral health history review.
**Risk Factors:**
- Poorly controlled blood sugar.
- Duration of diabetes.
- Smoking.
- Poor oral hygiene.
- Dry mouth conditions.
**Prevention:**
- Maintain optimal blood sugar levels.
- Practise good oral hygiene (brushing, flossing).
- Regular dental check-ups (at least twice a year).
- Quit smoking.
- Stay hydrated to prevent dry mouth.
==**Treatment:**
- Professional dental cleaning.
- Scaling and root planning for gum disease.
- Fluoride treatments for tooth sensitivity.
- Antibiotics for infections.
- Dental restorations as needed.

ACUTE COMPLICATIONS OF DIABETES
(DEVELOPS SUDDENLY)

Introduction:

Living with diabetes requires a vigilant eye on your health, as this condition comes with its set of challenges. Alongside the daily management of blood sugar levels, it's crucial to be aware of potential acute complications that can arise. Acute complications, while uncommon, can be serious and require immediate attention. Let's delve into some of the key acute complications of diabetes and how you can stay informed and proactive.

1. **Hypoglycemia (Low Blood Sugar):**(Most Important:Take immediate action)

- *Symptoms:* Shaking, sweating, confusion, dizziness, and irritability.

- *Action:* Consume a quick source of glucose, like fruit juice or glucose tablets.

2. **Hyperglycemia (High Blood Sugar):**(Not to worry immidiately)

- *Symptoms:* Excessive thirst, frequent urination, fatigue, and blurred vision.

- *Action:* Administer insulin as prescribed and reevaluate your meal plan.

3. **Diabetic Ketoacidosis (DKA):**

- *Symptoms:* Deep, laboured breathing, fruity-smelling breath, nausea, and vomiting.

- *Action:* Seek immediate medical attention, as DKA is a medical emergency that requires hospitalisation.

4. **Hyperosmolar Hyperglycemic State (HHS):**

- *Symptoms:* Extreme thirst, confusion, and high blood sugar levels.

- *Action:* Emergency medical attention is necessary, as HHS is a severe condition that can lead to dehydration and other complications.

Preventive Measures:

1. **Regular Monitoring:** Keep a close eye on your blood sugar levels through regular monitoring. Understanding your patterns helps in early detection.

2. **Medication Adherence:** Take prescribed medications as directed by your healthcare provider.

Skipping doses can contribute to fluctuations in blood sugar levels.

3. **Healthy Lifestyle Choices:** Maintain a balanced diet, engage in regular physical activity, and manage stress to promote overall well-being and diabetes control.

4. **Education and Support:** Stay informed about diabetes management. Attend educational sessions, support groups, and consult your healthcare team for guidance.

5. **Emergency Plan:** Develop an emergency plan with your healthcare provider. Know the signs and symptoms of acute complications and have a clear course of action.

Conclusion:

Being proactive in managing diabetes is key to preventing and mitigating acute complications. Regular communication with your healthcare team, a commitment to a healthy lifestyle, and prompt action in response to warning signs are vital elements of a comprehensive diabetes care plan. By staying informed and taking proactive steps, you empower yourself to navigate the challenges and complexities of diabetes, promoting a healthier and more vibrant life.

**Understanding Hypoglycemia in Diabetes: A Quick Guide**

Hypoglycemia, or low blood sugar, is a common concern for individuals managing diabetes. It occurs when blood glucose levels drop below normal, leading to various symptoms that require prompt attention.

**Symptoms:**
- Sweating
- Shakiness
- Irritability

- Rapid heartbeat
- Confusion
- Fatigue
- Dizziness
- Blurred vision
- Headache
- Hunger

**How to Confirm Hypoglycemia:**

Monitoring blood sugar levels through a glucose metre is the most effective way to confirm hypoglycemia. Typically, a reading below 70 mg/dL indicates low blood sugar.

**Common Causes:**

- Excessive insulin or medication dosage.
- Delayed or missed meals.
- Intense physical activity without adequate food intake.
- Alcohol consumption on an empty stomach.
- Changes in medication or insulin regimen without proper adjustment.

**Prevention:**

- Regularly monitor blood sugar levels.
- Maintain a consistent meal schedule.
- Eat a balanced diet with a mix of carbohydrates, protein, and healthy fats.
- Adjust medication dosages under healthcare supervision.
- Be mindful of alcohol consumption.

**Treatment:**

In the event of hypoglycemia, swift action is crucial:

1. Consume a fast-acting source of glucose, such as glucose tablets or gel, fruit juice, or regular soda.

2. Follow up with a snack containing carbohydrates and protein to stabilise blood sugar.

3. Regularly check blood sugar levels to ensure they return to the normal range.

It's vital for individuals with diabetes and their caregivers to be well-informed about the symptoms, confirmation methods, common causes, and appropriate actions for preventing and treating hypoglycemia. Timely and proper management ensures a safer and healthier diabetes journey. Always consult with healthcare professionals for personalised guidance.

# CHAPTER NINE

# DIABETES IN PREGNANCY

DEFINITION

**Gestational Diabetes Mellitus (GDM) is a type of diabetes that develops during pregnancy. It is characterised by elevated blood sugar levels, and it usually occurs around the 24th to 28th week of pregnancy when the body's insulin needs increase. GDM is a temporary condition, but if not properly managed, it can pose risks to both the mother and the baby. It is typically diagnosed through routine screening tests and requires careful monitoring and treatment during pregnancy to ensure the well-being of both the mother and the baby.**

Cause of GDM:

- Hormonal changes in pregnancy trigger GDM.

- Increased secretion of oestrogen, progesterone, human placental lactogen, prolactin, and cortisol.

- Normally, insulin levels counterbalance this diabetogenic status, but when insufficient, gestational diabetes occurs.

RISK FACTOR FOR DEVELOPMENT OF GDM:

1. **Obesity:** Women with a higher Body Mass Index (BMI) are at an increased risk.

2. **Age:** Women over the age of 25 are more likely to develop GDM.

3. **Family History:** A family history of diabetes, especially in parents or siblings.

4. **Previous Gestational Diabetes:** Women who have had gestational diabetes in a previous pregnancy.

5. **Ethnic Background:** Certain ethnic groups, including African-American, Hispanic, Native American, and Asian, have a higher risk.

6. **Polycystic Ovary Syndrome (PCOS):** Women with PCOS may have an elevated risk.

7. **Hypertension:** Pre-existing high blood pressure or gestational hypertension.

8. **Glucose Intolerance:** Pre-existing impaired glucose tolerance.

9. **Sedentary Lifestyle:** Lack of regular physical activity.

10. **Previous Large Birth Weight Baby:** Women who have previously given birth to a baby weighing 9 pounds or more.

11. **Poor Diet:** Unhealthy eating habits, including excessive consumption of refined sugars and low fibre intake.

12. **Multiple Pregnancies:** Women carrying twins or higher-order multiples.

It's important to note that the presence of one or more risk factors does not guarantee the development of gestational diabetes, and women without these risk factors can still develop GDM. Regular prenatal check-ups, screenings, and a healthy lifestyle are key to managing and minimising the risk of gestational diabetes.

EFFECTS OF GDM IN PREGNANCY IF NOT MANAGED PROPERLY

Gestational Diabetes Mellitus (GDM) can have various effects on the foetus, and it's important to manage the condition to minimise potential risks. Here are some of the effects of GDM on the foetus:

1. **Macrosomia:** GDM increases the risk of macrosomia, where the baby is born larger than average. This can lead to complications during delivery.

2. **Birth Injuries:** The risk of birth injuries, such as shoulder dystocia, is higher in babies born to mothers with uncontrolled GDM.

3. **Hypoglycemia:** Newborns may experience low blood sugar levels (hypoglycemia) after birth if the mother had GDM.

4. **Respiratory Distress Syndrome (RDS):** There is an increased risk of respiratory distress syndrome in babies born to mothers with GDM.

5. **Jaundice:** GDM can contribute to an increased risk of jaundice in the newborn.

6. **Risk of Obesity and Type 2 Diabetes:** Babies born to mothers with GDM may have a higher risk of developing obesity and type 2 diabetes later in life.

7. **Preterm Birth:** GDM increases the likelihood of preterm birth, which can lead to potential health complications for the baby.

8. **Stillbirth:** In severe cases or when GDM is poorly managed, there is an increased risk of stillbirth.

It's crucial for pregnant women with GDM to work closely with healthcare providers to manage blood sugar levels through lifestyle changes, diet, and sometimes medication. Proper management can significantly reduce the risks and promote a healthier outcome for both the mother and the baby.

DIAGNOSIS :

The International Association of Diabetes and Pregnancy Study Groups (IADPSG) provides specific diagnostic criteria for Gestational Diabetes Mellitus (GDM). These criteria are based on the results of the Oral Glucose Tolerance Test (OGTT). According to IADPSG, a diagnosis of GDM is made if any of the following glucose values are met or exceeded during the OGTT:

1. **Fasting Plasma Glucose (FPG):**
- Equal to or greater than 92 mg/dL (5.1 mmol/L).
2. **One-Hour Plasma Glucose:**
- Equal to or greater than 180 mg/dL (10.0 mmol/L).
3. **Two-Hour Plasma Glucose:**
- Equal to or greater than 153 mg/dL (8.5 mmol/L).

These criteria were developed to identify women at risk for adverse pregnancy outcomes related to hyperglycemia. It's important to note that these values represent stricter thresholds compared to previous criteria, aiming to capture more cases of hyperglycemia during pregnancy for improved management and outcomes.

Healthcare providers use these criteria to assess the results of the OGTT and make a diagnosis of GDM, allowing for timely intervention and management to reduce the associated risks for both the mother and the baby.

MANAGEMENT:

The management of Gestational Diabetes Mellitus (GDM) involves a combination of lifestyle modifications, blood sugar monitoring, and, in some cases, medication. Here is an overview of the key aspects of GDM management:

1. **Blood Sugar Monitoring:**
- Regular monitoring of blood sugar levels is crucial.
- Home glucose monitoring with a glucometer to track fasting and postprandial levels.

2. **Healthy Diet:**
The dietary approach for gestational diabetes is akin to general diabetes management, with a few specific considerations:
- Work with a registered dietitian to create a balanced meal plan.
- Emphasise whole grains, fruits, vegetables, lean proteins, and healthy fats.
- Monitor carbohydrate intake to help regulate blood sugar levels.
- **Caloric Intake:**
- Provide 30 to 40 kilocalories per kilogram per day to the mother.
- Consult a dietitian for personalised guidance.
(YOU CAN MAKE YOUR DIET ACCORDING TO THE DIET ADVICEGIVEN IN THE BEGINNING OF THE BOOK)
- **Nutritional Maintenance:**
- Ensure proper nutritional maintenance alongside caloric intake.
- Collaborate with a dietitian to manage gestational diabetes effectively.
3. **Regular Physical Activity:**
- Engage in moderate-intensity exercise, as recommended by healthcare providers.
4. **Medication (if needed):**
- Insulin: For some women, insulin therapy may be prescribed to control blood sugar level as it is the safest treatment available for tretatment of GDM
- Oral Medications: In certain cases, oral medications may be considered, although insulin is often the preferred choice during pregnancy.
5. **Regular Prenatal Check-ups:**

- Attend scheduled prenatal visits to monitor both maternal and foetal health.

- Discuss any concerns or changes in symptoms with healthcare providers.

7. **Education and Support:**

- Receive education on self-care, blood sugar monitoring, and the importance of adherence to the management plan.

- Seek support from healthcare providers, diabetes educators, and support groups.

8. **Delivery Planning:**

- Collaborate with healthcare providers to plan for a safe and healthy delivery.

- Monitoring blood sugar levels during labour.

9. **Postpartum Care:**

- Continue blood sugar monitoring after delivery.

- Assess the risk of developing type 2 diabetes in the future.

Effective management of GDM aims to maintain blood sugar levels within target ranges to minimise risks for both the mother and the baby. It requires a collaborative effort between the woman, healthcare providers, and a multidisciplinary team to ensure the best outcomes during and after pregnancy.

IMPORTANT POINTS TO NOTE FOR GDM PATIENTS:

In pregnancy, GDM, or gestational diabetes mellitus, occurs when diabetes is diagnosed for the first time between the 24th and 28th weeks of pregnancy. This is distinct from pre-gestational diabetes mellitus, or pre-GDM, where diabetes is diagnosed before pregnancy begins.

Here's a breakdown:

- **Two Types of Diabetes in Pregnancy:**

- GDM (Gestational Diabetes Mellitus)

- Usually mild and of shorter duration.

- Often returns to normal blood sugar levels after delivery.

- PGDM (Pre-gestational Diabetes Mellitus)

- Persists for a longer duration.

- Present before pregnancy, requiring insulin for a few weeks post-delivery.

- **Unified Management Approach:**

- Despite differences, the management for both types is generally the same.

- **Monitoring GDM:**

- Critical part of management.

- Home monitoring with a glucometer, checking blood sugar four times daily.

- Fasting levels around 90 mg, post meals around 120 mg per deciliter.

- Patient records and WhatsApps results every 3 days (frequency depends upon Patients condition)

- Adjustments to insulin doses made to maintain normal blood sugar levels.

- **Communication During Pregnancy:**

- Clinic visits are minimised, with most interactions occurring via phone or WhatsApp.

- Patients provided with a record sheet to track blood sugar levels.

Understanding these distinctions and the importance of consistent monitoring allows for effective management of gestational diabetes during pregnancy.

**Myths & Mistakes:**

**Facing gestational diabetes mellitus (GDM) can be daunting for expectant mothers, leading some to consider aborting the pregnancy out of fear. It's essential**

to remember that the gift of a child is a precious one, bestowed upon you by God. While managing GDM might seem challenging initially, rest assured that many women with gestational diabetes deliver their babies happily, encountering minimal complications throughout their pregnancy. Despite the theoretical complications that may be written in books, the practical occurrence of complications is relatively low.

Addressing common concerns:

- **Risk to Newborn's Health:**

- GDM or pre-GDM doesn't immediately increase the risk of diabetes in newborns.

- However, there's a potential future risk of diabetes in later stages of life, a prevalent concern in today's society.

- **Birth Defects:**

- Properly managing diabetes reduces the chances of deformities.

- Regular antenatal check-ups and anomaly scans during pregnancy help detect any abnormalities, allowing for timely action.

- **Insulin Use:**

- In most cases, gestational diabetes resolves after delivery, and no lifelong treatment is needed.

- Insulin use is rare post-delivery, occurring only in exceptional cases.

- **Controlling GDM:**

- GDM can often be managed with diet or a combination of diet and medication.

- Insulin may be required if blood sugar levels aren't adequately controlled through diet and medication during pregnancy.

- **Mode of Delivery:**

- The choice of the delivery mode typically rests with the doctor.

- Patient involvement in this decision is discouraged.

- **Post-Delivery Monitoring:**

- After delivery, an oral glucose tolerance test (OGTT) is recommended after 6 weeks.

- If not possible, fasting and postprandial blood sugar tests are advised.

- Regular monitoring at six-month intervals throughout life is crucial.

Navigating gestational diabetes involves addressing fears, understanding the risks, and following medical advice to ensure a healthy pregnancy and delivery.

Q&A

**Reversing Gestational Diabetes:**

Gestational diabetes is a temporary stage, and the cautious approach is essential. While it's not advisable to risk decreasing blood sugar without medication or insulin, there are steps you can take:

- **Diet Control:**

- Monitor and control your diet.

- Consult a healthcare professional to tailor your diet plan.

- **Medication and Insulin:**

- Take prescribed medications and insulin, if necessary.

- Adjustments will be made based on regular monitoring.

- If blood sugar responds well to medication and insulin, dosages may be gradually reduced.

- The goal is to achieve blood sugar control .

** Gestational Diabetes is dangerous:**

Gestational diabetes, when managed properly, is not inherently dangerous. A combination of a well-regulated diet, medication, and frequent checkups ensures a safe pregnancy.

Remember, the key is a balanced and controlled approach, involving diet, medication, and regular checkups for a healthy pregnancy journey.

# CHAPTER TEN

# DISEASES ASSOCIATED WITH DIABETES

These are the diseases which are closely associated with most of the Dabetes patient and If one is present other comes along with that ,sooner or later.

**HYPERTENSION**

There are many diseases associated with DM that should be managed properly to prevent complications. One such condition is hypertension, commonly known as high blood pressure, a significant risk factor for heart disease and stroke. Often referred to as the "silent killer" due to its asymptomatic nature, hypertension can lead to severe health complications.

There are many diseases associated with DM that should be managed properly to prevent complications. One such condition is hypertension, commonly known as high blood pressure, a significant risk factor for heart disease and stroke. Often referred to as the "silent killer" due to its asymptomatic nature, hypertension can lead to severe health complications.

**Symptoms:**
- Hypertension is often asymptomatic.
- Severe cases may cause headaches, shortness of breath, or nosebleeds.

**Signs:**
- High blood pressure readings during regular check-ups.

**Diagnosis:**
- Blood pressure measurements (systolic/diastolic).
- Multiple readings to confirm diagnosis.
- Additional tests to assess potential organ damage.

**Risk Factors:**
- Age (risk increases with age).
- Family history of hypertension.
- Obesity or being overweight.
- Lack of physical activity.
- Unhealthy diet (high in salt, low in potassium).
- Smoking.
- Excessive alcohol consumption.
- Stress.

**Prevention:**
- Adopt a heart-healthy diet (low salt, rich in fruits and vegetables).
- Engage in regular physical activity.
- Maintain a healthy weight.
- Limit alcohol intake.
- Quit smoking.
- Manage stress through relaxation techniques.

**Treatment:**
- Lifestyle modifications (diet, exercise).
- Medications as prescribed by healthcare professionals.
- Regular monitoring of blood pressure.

- Decrease the use of extra salt intake in the form of snacks, fast food, etc.

- Hypertension is often asymptomatic.

- Severe cases may cause headaches, shortness of breath, or nosebleeds.

**Diagnosis:**

- Blood pressure measurements (systolic/diastolic).

- Multiple readings to confirm diagnosis.

- Additional tests to assess potential organ damage.

**Prevention:**

- Adopt a heart-healthy diet (low salt, rich in fruits and vegetables).

- Engage in regular physical activity.

- Maintain a healthy weight.

- Limit alcohol intake.

- Quit smoking.

- Manage stress through relaxation techniques.

**Treatment:**

- Lifestyle modifications (diet, exercise).

- Medications as prescribed by healthcare professionals.

- Regular monitoring of blood pressure.

- Decrease the use of extra salt intake in the form of snacks, fast food, etc.

**Dos and Don'ts:**

- **Do:** Follow prescribed medications consistently.

- **Do:** Monitor blood pressure at home if advised.

- **Do:** Maintain a healthy lifestyle with balanced nutrition.

- **Don't:** Exceed recommended sodium intake.

- **Don't:** Skip medications without consulting a healthcare provider.

- **Don't:** Ignore regular check-ups and blood pressure screenings.

Hypertension is manageable with a proactive approach to lifestyle and medical care. Regular monitoring and adherence to prescribed treatments play a vital role in preventing complications and maintaining overall health.

**FATTY LIVER (NAFLD)**

**Importance:**

- Diabetes increases the risk of Non-Alcoholic Fatty Liver Disease (NAFLD), which can lead to liver inflammation, scarring, and ultimately hepatic failure.

**Symptoms:**

- Fatigue.

- Abdominal discomfort.

- Unexplained weight loss.

- Jaundice (rare in NAFLD).

- Diagnosed in routine examinations.

**Diagnosis:**

- Blood tests for elevated liver enzymes.

- Imaging studies (ultrasound, CT scan, MRI).

- Fibroscan.

- Liver biopsy in some cases.

**Risk Factors:**

- Poorly controlled blood sugar.

- Obesity.

- High blood pressure.

- High cholesterol.

- Insulin resistance.

**Prevention:**

- Maintain optimal blood sugar levels.

- Adopt a healthy, balanced diet.

- Engage in regular physical activity.

- Manage weight through lifestyle changes.

- Limit alcohol consumption.

**Treatment:**

- Lifestyle modifications (diet, exercise) are crucial.

- Medications to manage diabetes and associated conditions.

- Weight loss interventions.

- Monitoring and managing cardiovascular risk factors.

- Regular follow-up with healthcare providers.

Managing diabetes is crucial in preventing and mitigating the impact of NAFLD. Adopting a healthy lifestyle and regular medical check-ups play a key role in maintaining liver health for individuals with diabetes.

## HIGH CHOLESTEROL OR DYSLIPIDEMIA

**Importance:**

- Dyslipidemia involves abnormal lipid (cholesterol and triglycerides) levels, posing a significant risk for cardiovascular diseases, including heart attacks and strokes.

**Symptoms:**

- Dyslipidemia typically shows no noticeable symptoms, with health issues becoming apparent only when complications arise.

**Signs:**

- Detected through blood tests measuring cholesterol and triglyceride levels.

**Diagnosis:**

- Lipid profile blood test assessing total cholesterol, LDL, HDL, and triglycerides.

**Risk Factors:**

- Unhealthy diet high in saturated and trans fats.

- Lack of physical activity.

- Obesity.

- Smoking.

- Excessive alcohol consumption.

- Genetics and family history of dyslipidemia.

**Prevention:**

- Adopt a heart-healthy diet (low in saturated and trans fats).
- Engage in regular physical activity.
- Maintain a healthy weight.
- Avoid smoking and limit alcohol intake.
**Treatment:**
- Lifestyle modifications (diet, exercise).
- Medications (statins, fibrates) as prescribed.
- Regular monitoring of lipid levels.
**Dos and Don'ts:**
- **Do:** Follow prescribed medications consistently; many patients stop due to the absence of symptoms.
- **Do:** Embrace a diet rich in fruits, vegetables, and whole grains.
- **Do:** Engage in regular physical activity.
- **Don't:** Consume excessive saturated and trans fats.
- **Don't:** Neglect regular check-ups and lipid profile screenings.
- **Don't:** Discontinue medications without consulting a healthcare provider.

Managing dyslipidemia is crucial for cardiovascular health. Positive lifestyle choices and adherence to medical advice significantly reduce the risk of heart-related complications associated with lipid disorders. Regular check-ups play a key role in overall well-being.

NOTE: According to guidelines many patients of Diabetes and high Blood pressure are given cholesterol lowering drugs without any increase in Blood cholesterol level ,In such cases advice is to be followed strictly even without any doubts as advised by your physician because Lowering cholesterol level prevents further development of heart disease in future.

**OBESITY**

**Importance:**
- Obesity, marked by excess body weight, significantly increases the risk of health problems like heart disease, diabetes, and certain cancers.
**Symptoms:**
- Often no specific symptoms.
- Health issues may arise gradually over time.
**Signs:**
- Body Mass Index (BMI) of 30 or higher indicates obesity.
**Diagnosis:**
- BMI measurement.
- Assessment of overall health and lifestyle.
**Risk Factors:**
- Unhealthy diet high in calories and processed foods.
- Sedentary lifestyle with little physical activity.
- Genetics and family history.
- Psychological factors (stress, depression).
- Certain medical conditions and medications.
**Prevention:**
- Adopt a balanced, nutritious diet.
- Engage in regular physical activity.
- Maintain a healthy lifestyle with sufficient sleep.
- Address emotional well-being and stress.
**Treatment:**
- Lifestyle modifications (diet, exercise).
- Behavioural therapy and counselling.
- Medications (in some cases).
- Bariatric surgery (for severe obesity).
**Dos and Don'ts:**
- **Do:** Prioritise a balanced, portion-controlled diet.
- **Do:** Incorporate regular physical activity into daily life.

- **Do:** Seek support from healthcare professionals or support groups and make a long term goal to treat Obesity.
- **Don't:** Rely on crash diets or extreme weight loss methods.
- **Don't:** Neglect mental and emotional health.
- **Don't:** Avoid seeking professional help if needed and Don't try to treat yourself.

Managing obesity requires a holistic approach that combines healthy lifestyle choices, behavioural changes, and, if necessary, medical interventions. By addressing the root causes and making sustainable changes, individuals can improve their overall health and reduce the risks associated with obesity. Regular check-ups and collaboration with healthcare providers play a crucial role in achieving and maintaining a healthy weight.

# UNDERSTANDING DIABETES REVERSAL

**1. Definition of Reversal:**

- Reversal signifies a substantial improvement in blood sugar control.

- It implies meeting criteria where the individual no longer fits the diagnosis of diabetes.

- Reversal is achievable primarily for those with type 2 diabetes, but it may not be applicable to everyone.

**2. Eligibility for Reversal:**

- Typically considered for individuals with type 2 diabetes.

- Less likely for those with type 1 diabetes, which is an autoimmune condition.

- Reversal is closely linked to lifestyle factors like diet and physical activity.

**3. Criteria for Reversal:**

a. **Blood Sugar Levels:**

- Involves maintaining normal or near-normal blood glucose levels without medication.

b. **Weight Management:**

- Achieving and sustaining a healthy weight is crucial for improved insulin sensitivity.

c. **Lifestyle Changes:**

- Significant alterations, including a balanced diet, regular exercise, and stress management.

**4. Myths About Reversal:**

a. **Myth: Reversal is a One-Time Event:**

- Reversal is an ongoing process, and maintaining lifestyle changes is essential for sustained results.

b. **Myth: Medications Are Always Required:**

- While some may need medications, others can achieve reversal through lifestyle changes alone.

c. **Myth: Only Severe Cases Can Reverse:**

- Reversal is possible at various stages, and early intervention often yields better results.

**5. Actual Meaning of Reversal:**

a. **Reduced Medication Dependency:**

- Successful reversal often leads to reduced or eliminated need for certain medications.

b. **Improved A1C Levels:**

- Confirmed by lowered Haemoglobin A1C levels reflecting improved blood sugar control.

c. **Enhanced Quality of Life:**

- Beyond medical markers, reversal results in increased energy, improved mood, and decreased risk of complications.

**Conclusion:**

- Reversing diabetes is feasible with a holistic approach.

- Involves lifestyle changes, weight management, and sometimes, medication adjustments.

- Debunking myths is essential for a clearer understanding of the achievable goal of a diabetes-free life.

# Conclusion

As we approach the final pages of the "THE DIABETES HANDBOOK," I find myself reflecting on the incredible journey we've undertaken together through the intricate landscape of diabetes. Our mission was simple: to demystify the complexities surrounding diabetes and equip you, the reader, with the tools and knowledge to navigate this path to wellness. Here are the key pillars we explored:

1. **Diet Control:**

In the culinary labyrinth of diabetes management, we navigated through the importance of mindful eating. By understanding the impact of different food choices on blood sugar levels, we aimed to empower you to make informed decisions and create a diet that not only sustains but nourishes.

2. **Exercise:**

From the simplicity of a brisk walk to the intricacies of tailored workout routines, we delved into the transformative power of exercise. Physical activity is not just a routine; it's a companion in the journey to better health, helping to manage blood sugar levels and fostering overall well-being.

3. **Regular Medicines:**

Medication, when understood and embraced as a partner, becomes a potent ally in the fight against diabetes. We explored the nuances of various medications, emphasising the importance of adherence to prescribed regimens for effective blood sugar control.

4. **Regular Blood Sugar and Other Checkups:**

Monitoring is the compass that keeps us on course. We discussed the significance of regular blood sugar checks and other essential screenings. By embracing these routine evaluations, you've equipped yourself with the knowledge needed to respond to your body's signals and make informed decisions.

5. **Regular Doctor Checkup:**

Your healthcare provider is not just a consultant; they are a guide in this expedition. We highlighted the significance of regular checkups, fostering a partnership between you and your healthcare team. Through open communication, you can address concerns, tweak strategies, and ensure your journey remains on the path to success.

As you close the cover of this handbook, I invite you to share your thoughts and experiences. Your feedback is invaluable, not only to us but to others who may embark on this journey in the future. Connect with us on our various social media handles, share your insights, and let the community thrive. If you purchased the book through Amazon or Notion Press, consider leaving a review. Your words have the power to guide and inspire others on their own quest for wellness.

I want to express my heartfelt gratitude for being a part of this journey. Your commitment to learning and understanding diabetes demonstrates a resilience that is truly commendable. Together, we've turned the pages of knowledge, and I hope this book serves as a beacon of insight and support on your ongoing voyage towards a healthier and happier life.

Wishing you wellness and vitality,

Dr Shiv Kumar Lath,MBBS,MD,FEAC

# Connect Through Below Mentioned Link With Us

- Explore Dr. Lath Polyclinic on Google: [Google Page](https://g.page/r/CfF9aWzdVvOHEAE)

- Consult Online with Dr. Shiv Kumar Lath on Lybrate: [Lybrate](https://www.lybrate.com/jharsuguda/doctor/dr-shiv-kumar-lath-general-physician)

- Facebook Page: [Diabetes Jharsuguda](https://www.facebook.com/diabetesjharsuguda?mibextid=ZbWKwL)

- Instagram: [Defeat Diabetes India](https://instagram.com/defeatdiabetesindia?igshid=MzNlNGNkZWQ4Mg==)

- YouTube Channel: [Patient Education](https://youtube.com/@patienteducation2101)

- Share your feedback on Just Dial: [Rate Us](http://jsdl.in/JR-RTHQHH11786051)

- Consult online directly by calling in numbers:9040881281,9438226633

**send your reviews directly to us at** drsklath@gmail.com

Your engagement is important to us!

**IF YOU LIKE THE BOOK AND WANT TO BUY ONE ,YOU CAN VISIT THE NOTION PRESS WEBSITE AND SEARCH FOR THE BOOK AND FIND UNDERSTANDING DIABETES AND BUY IT ONLINE DIRECTLY FROM THERE OR YOU CAN CONTACT OUR CLINIC IN JHARSUGUDA AT 9040881281,9438226633**

www.ingramcontent.com/pod-product-compliance
Lightning Source LLC
Chambersburg PA
CBHW051606180726
47991CB00027B/2351